SEMANTICS OF THE ENGLISH SUBJUNCTIVE

In this book Francis James develops his theory that the English subjunctive has one meaning. Explaining how modality expresses the relation between a representation and what is represented, James compares the subjunctive to a "blueprint," a plan of what the architect intends the world to match; and the indicative to an artist's sketch of the same building, a "record" to match the world. The subjunctive thus signifies the practical world-to-match-words modality, and the indicative, the theoretical words-to-match-world modality.

In individual chapters, the author gives a unified account of current and earlier uses of the present and past subjunctive and comments on how historical changes have affected the syntax of the moods. He extends his argument to demonstrate how the theory of modality can be applied to other modal forms in English and to moods in other languages.

Like works on such other verbal categories as aspect and futurity, the theory of the subjunctive has interest for historical and theoretical linguists, philosophers, students of cognitive science and literary theory.

FRANCIS JAMES is a member of the English department at the University of British Columbia.

SEMANTICS

OF THE

ENGLISH

SUBJUNCTIVE

Francis James

UNIVERSITY OF BRITISH COLUMBIA PRESS

VANCOUVER 1986

SEMANTICS OF THE ENGLISH SUBJUNCTIVE

Second Printing, December, 1987

This book has been published with the help of a grant
from the Canadian Federation for the Humanities.

Canadian Cataloguing in Publication Data

James, Francis, 1950–
    Semantics of the English Subjunctive

    Bibliography: p.
    Includes index.
    ISBN 0-7748-0255-3

    1. English language - Subjunctive.
2. English language - Mood. I. Title.
PE1290.J34 1986   425   C86-091262-0

International Standard Book Number 0-7748-0255-3

Printed in Canada

CONTENTS

PREFACE

This study in the semantics of the English moods with special reference to the subjunctive develops a theory of modality based on a hypothesis that there is a fundamental distinction between two ways that any representation, linguistic or otherwise, can be intended: these are (1) as a record, something which matches states of affairs in the world, or (2) as a blueprint, something which states of affairs are to match. It argues that the subjunctive signifies the manner of representation comparable to a blueprint. It gives a unified account of both current and earlier uses of the present and past subjunctive and comments on how historical changes have affected the syntax of the moods. It also suggests how the theory of modality can be extended to other modal forms in English and to moods in other languages, with brief illustration from French and Greek.

I would like to thank Fred Bowers, Laurel Brinton, Hervé Curat, Walter Hirtle, Andrea Lunsford, Jo Powell, Bruce Redwine, Alain Renoir, Gernot Wieland, and the readers for UBC Press and the Canadian Federation for the Humanities for reading earlier versions of the manuscript and offering valuable comments and suggestions. I would also like to thank my research assistant, Tom Friedman, for finding and checking primary sources for examples cited in the text.

My greatest debt is to Julian Boyd, whose theory of modality has inspired this work.

1

INTRODUCTION

The subjunctive mood poses two difficult problems for Modern English grammar. One is the syntactic problem of whether it is still justifiable to regard the subjunctive as a mood, that is, as a system of inflections on verbs, contrasting with two other moods, the indicative and the imperative. This problem does not arise in earlier English, where the subjunctive still has a large number of phonologically distinctive forms and is productive in many uses. A second problem is whether the subjunctive has, or did have, a single basic meaning which characterizes it, distinguishes it from the other moods, and unifies its uses. Although the syntactic problem is discussed, the semantic problem is the focus of this study. I argue that the subjunctive does have a basic meaning, and I attempt to describe this meaning within a general theory of modality. Although I concentrate on the subjunctive, the theory developed in describing its meaning will be applicable to other moods and to other modal forms, both in English and in other languages.[1]

1.1 SUBJUNCTIVE FORMS

The term 'subjunctive' throughout will refer to a grammatical form, not a meaning. In this and other matters of terminology I follow the usage of historical grammars.[2] These grammars describe inflections on verbs in Indo-European languages as specifying elements from five separate categories, person, number, tense, mood, and voice. All five categories presumably occur in Germanic, but voice is lost before Old English. The other four categories remain in Old English, and they, or reflexes of them, remain in present-day English, though historical changes make their status somewhat doubtful. It is convenient, and realistic, to think of each element of each category as a morpheme, a minimal meaning-bearing form. Each element, though a single grammatical form, has variant phonological forms, or allomorphs. Reconstruction shows that the Indo-European mood (the optative) from which the English subjunctive descends has three such variants, these being -*jē-*, -*i-*, and -*i-*.[3] In their development from Indo-European into English these original variants produce new variants and so create much diversity among the phonological forms which signal the grammatical form, but in all the early Germanic languages, the subjunctive is clearly distinguishable from other grammatical forms of the verb. (Sample paradigms of Old English verbs are provided in Appendix A.)

Some verb forms in present-day English can still be clearly identified as subjunctive (or as survivals of the earlier subjunctive). In the present tense the verb *be* has subjunctive and indicative forms which are distinct from each other in all persons and numbers. Compare the inflected forms of *be,* subjunctive and indicative respectively, in the sentences,

They prefer that it be so.

They know that it is so.

Subjunctive and indicative forms are distinctive in all other verbs (save the modal auxiliaries) in the present tense, third person singular. Compare the forms of the verb *come* in the sentences,

They prefer that she come.

They know that she comes.

In the past tense only the verb *be* has distinctive subjunctive and indicative forms. Compare the sentences,

They wish that he were here.

They know that he was here.

When subjunctive and indicative forms are not phonologically distinguishable, other criteria apply. The subjunctive cannot follow a sequence of tenses, so that, as a past tense counterpart of *They prefer that it be so,* only the first of the following two sentences is acceptable:

They preferred that it be so.

*They preferred that it were so.

The indicative can follow a sequence of tenses, so that, as a past tense counterpart of *They know that it is so,* either of the following is acceptable:

They knew that it is so.

They knew that it was so.

In negative sentences, the present subjunctive does not require the auxiliary *do* and the word *not* precedes the finite verb, but the present indicative does require the auxiliary and *not* follows the finite verb. Compare the sentences,

They prefer that you not come early.

They know that you do not come early.

In conditional sentences, past subjunctive *were* allows subject-verb inversion in the protasis, but past indicative *was* does not. Only the first of the following two sentences is acceptable:

Were she allowed to come, she would.

*Was she allowed to come, she did.

The verbs *should* and *had,* which have no phonologically distinguishable subjunctive and indicative forms, also allow subject-verb inversion, as in the sentences,

Should she be allowed to come, she would.

Had she been allowed to come, she would have.

No other verbs, except perhaps *could,* have past tense forms which allow inversion in this context.

In Old English, subjunctive forms are phonologically distinguishable from imperative forms and from infinitive forms, but none of these forms remain distinguishable in present-day English. Other criteria, however, can still be applied to distinguish the forms. The verb *come* is phonologically identical in the following three sentences, although from a historical point of view *come* is a subjunctive in the first, an imperative in the second, and an infinitive in the third:

I prefer that you come.

Come. (You, come.)

I want you to come.

The imperative allows deletion of the subject, or special vocative intonation for the subject, but the subjunctive allows neither. The infinitive occurs with a preceding particle *to* or with a preceding verb (a modal auxiliary, for example), but the subjunctive occurs with neither. The phonological identity of the three forms is very recent, and the syntactic environments in which the forms occur remain markedly different.[4]

1.2 THE SYNTACTIC PROBLEM IN PRESENT-DAY ENGLISH

The non-distinctiveness of subjunctive forms, and indeed all inflectional forms of the verb save the two tenses, which remain clearly marked, creates problems for the syntactic analysis of present-day English. It is difficult to determine whether the few contrasting forms that remain in the language are sufficient to maintain the earlier inflectional system, and even if we assume that the subjunctive still survives as a mood, we must observe that its use is much more restricted now than in earlier times. I take the traditional view that its declining use results largely from the decreasing distinctiveness of its phonological forms, which in turn results from the leveling of unstressed final syllables in Middle English.[5] It seems that as inflections are leveled, non-distinctive forms are interpreted as indicative wherever possible. We can only speculate about why this should be so, but perhaps the reason is that the indicative has always been more frequent overall and often more frequent in uses which have allowed either mood. With a trend underway to interpret non-distinctive forms as indicative, we can assume that wherever the indicative was semantically inappropriate, speakers would try to find substitutes for the non-distinctive subjunctive in order to avoid confusion or misinterpretation.

The syntactic problem in present-day English, insofar as it is a special problem of the subjunctive and not the very general problem of how to identify and categorize inflectional or periphrastic forms of verbs, is caused by the subjunctive's gradual obsolescence. Alternative syntactic analyses of any one standard national dialect are surely possible, and there is much dialectal variation. For instance, the present subjunctive is nearly obsolete in conditional clauses introduced by *if,* as in the sentence,

They will not go on if that be so.

We might therefore analyze it as a stylistic variant of the indicative, providing an archaic touch but not differing from it in any other way. In adverbial clauses not introduced by *if,* the subjunctive is also nearly obsolete. Sentences introduced by such clauses as *come what may* or *be it so or otherwise* still occur in written English, but such clauses are now probably best described as idioms. Again, we might analyze the subjunctive as a stylistic variant of the indicative, noting that inversion of word order serves the same function as a subordinating conjunction. The present subjunctive in independent clauses, where it usually implies wish, is restricted to fossilized constructions like the following:

So be it.

God save the queen.

Like conditional clauses with inverted word order, these are probably best described as idioms. We might analyze the subjunctive in independent clauses as a stylistic variant of *let* or *may* with the infinitive, which occur in sentences like *Let it be so, May it be so,* or *May God save the queen.*

The past subjunctive is likewise nearly obsolete in conditional clauses, though its use is somewhat more frequent than use of the present subjunctive. Again, we might analyze it as a variant form of the indicative. We might be particularly inclined to do so since the past subjunctive is only distinct from the past indicative in the first and third person singular of the verb *be.* This past subjunctive form *were* in object clauses after the word *wish,* as in conditional clauses, occurs frequently, but mainly in educated use and in formal contexts, so we might regard it too as a stylistic or dialectal variant. Ignoring obsolescent uses, we are left with only one productive use of the present subjunctive, the use in noun clauses, and we must observe that this use is more common in North America than in Britain. Moreover, since the present subjunctive is no longer phonologically distinct from the imperative or the infinitive (taking the infinitive without the particle *to*), we might analyze it as belonging to one of these, or we might analyze all three as a single form.

The syntactic problem has little bearing on the semantic problem of distinguishing the subjunctive's meaning from the meanings of the other moods and reconciling its uses. I grant that it is possible to treat subjunctives in obsolescent uses as exceptional forms in present-day English, not having meaning independent of the meanings they acquire in special constructions, where they can be analyzed as idiomatic variants of more regular forms. In fact I doubt that modern speakers unschooled in grammar associate the obsolescent subjunctives with the productive present subjunctive that occurs in noun clauses. However, the subjunctive has not always been obsolescent in these uses, and we must distinguish the present subjunctive from the indicative in noun clauses in any case. Therefore, I temporarily set aside the problems created by recent historical changes and analyze the subjunctive in its earlier range of uses.

1.3 THE SEMANTIC PROBLEM OF RECONCILING USES

The subjunctive is particularly interesting from a semantic point of view because it is particularly difficult to analyze. Combined with the present tense, it has uses of such range that they seem to overlap, on one hand, with uses of the imperative and, on the other, with uses of the indicative. In noun clauses, for example, the choice of subjunctive or indicative produces a clear contrast in meaning. Compare the effects of the inflectional form of the verb *be* in the sentences,

They insist that she be there.

They insist that she is there.

The first of these sentences has imperative force, as changing the pronouns illustrates clearly. Compare the sentences,

I insist that you be there.

Be there. (I insist.)

If we assume that the old distinctions of mood remain intact, the verb *be* in the first sentence is subjunctive, while *be* in the second is imperative. In conditional clauses, on the other hand, the choice of subjunctive or indicative produces no clear contrast in meaning. Compare the forms of the verb *be* in the sentences,

If she be there, you will see her.

If she is there, you will see her.

The only apparent difference between these two sentences is that the first is archaic. Subjunctive *be* does not seem to have the imperative force it has in object clauses, and instead it seems semantically comparable to indicative *is*.

Combining past tense and subjunctive mood produces an effect strikingly different from the effect of combining past tense and indicative mood. The effect of tense can be illustrated in both noun clauses and conditional clauses. Compare the noun clauses of the sentences,

They wish that she were there.

They know that she was there.

And compare the conditional clauses of the sentences,

If she were there, they would see her.

If she was there, they saw her.

Combined with the indicative, the tense has temporal significance, but combined with the subjunctive, it does not.

The difficulty of reconciling uses of the present subjunctive with each other and with uses of the past subjunctive makes the subjunctive a good point of departure for a semantic study of mood, for the analysis of it raises issues which might be overlooked in the analysis of the apparently more homogeneous imperative or indicative. The analysis presented here focuses on the uses illustrated above, one of which is still productive and four of which have survived into the twentieth century in fixed constructions. Three are uses of the present subjunctive, these being uses in independent clauses expressing wish, as in *So be it,* in noun clauses expressing demand or desire, as in *They insist that it be so,* and in adverb clauses expressing open condition, as in *They will not go on if it be so.* The remaining two are uses of the past subjunctive, these being uses in noun clauses expressing idle wish, as in *They wish that it were so,* and in adverb clauses expressing counterfactual condition, as in *They would not go on if it were so.* The decline of the subjunctive is itself of interest, and so surviving uses are placed in historical perspective. The present subjunctive once occurred far more extensively than now, and important earlier uses considered are those in object clauses after emotion words expressing hope, fear, or belief and words of saying or asking and in adverb clauses expressing concession, time, or purpose. The past subjunctive once occurred in the same variety of uses as the present subjunctive, and I consider uses in independent clauses, particularly in exclamations and in the apodosis of conditional sentences, and in dependent clauses like those in which the present subjunctive occurs. The historical perspective gives the analysis greater generality. Losing uses over time, the subjunctive has nevertheless retained its basic meaning, and by considering older uses we can develop a semantic description of the subjunctive that applies at all periods of the language. Furthermore, earlier English, in allowing the subjunctive a far wider distribution, corresponds more closely to other languages that have a subjunctive or optative mood, so considering older uses will facilitate comparison between languages.

1.4 TOPICS AND DATA

The analysis proceeds in this order. Chapter 2 develops a theory of modality with reference to the present subjunctive, and with this theory reconciles the present subjunctive's current and earlier uses. Chapter 3 analyzes the past subjunctive, showing the combined semantic effect of its two elements, subjunctive mood and past tense, and reconciling its current and earlier uses. Chapter 4 describes how grammatical forms that have replaced the subjunctive are semantically similar and so fitting substitutes and takes up the question of syntax again, exploring the possibility of analyzing English as having a present subjunctive but no past subjunctive or as having only two moods, imperative and indicative. Chapter 5 very briefly considers extensions of the theory of modality to moods in other languages, particularly Modern French and Classical Attic Greek.

Example sentences from earlier periods of English are taken from F. Th. Visser's *An Historical Syntax of the English Language.* Visser supplies a wealth of examples for each type of construction discussed, and so is a good source for additional data. Whenever possible, I have checked the primary sources for sentences cited in Visser, and I have quoted the sentences and their immediate context in Appendix B. Full bibliographic references for primary sources are given in a separate list at the end of the appendix.

2

SEMANTICS OF THE PRESENT SUBJUNCTIVE

Both the present subjunctive and the present indicative occur in independent clauses, as in *So be it* and *It is so,* in object clauses, as in *They insist that it be so* and *They insist that it is so,* and in conditional clauses, as in *They will not go on if it be so* and *They will not go on if it is so.* The problem is that the choice of mood produces a clear contrast in meaning in the independent and object clauses, but no clear contrast in the conditional clauses. How then do we describe the semantics of the present subjunctive? In this chapter I argue that the subjunctive signifies one of two basic modalities. I explain the apparent differences in its meaning with an analysis that distinguishes it semantically from the indicative and the imperative and also reconciles its disparate current uses and its earlier uses.

2.1 POSSIBLE AMBIGUITY OF THE PRESENT SUBJUNCTIVE

An alternative approach would avoid the problem'of reconciling its uses altogether. If we take the subjunctive in conditional clauses to be a stylistic variant of the indicative in present-day English, then we might say that it is ambiguous, for the subjunctive's meaning in object clauses contrasts with the indicative's in a way that is more than stylistic. For earlier English, before obsolescence creates stylistic differences, the ambiguity would be even clearer: the subjunctive would be synonymous with the indicative (or nearly so) in one of its meanings but would contrast with it sharply in the other. Considering the subjunctive to be ambiguous, we might try to avoid the problem of reconciling its uses simply by saying that they need not be reconciled. Ambiguity accounts for the different uses. But this solution creates other problems which are equally difficult. How would we describe the semantics of the indicative? Is it too ambiguous, with one meaning in conditional clauses and another in object clauses? And what about independent clauses? Do either or both the subjunctive and the indicative have a third meaning in independent clauses?

Another difficulty in calling the subjunctive ambiguous is to describe the ambiguity. Surely the ambiguity is not homonymy. To say that what is traditionally referred to as the subjunctive is actually two moods, let us call them the optative and the conditional, which are semantically unrelated and only by chance have the same phonological form, is highly implausible. If we maintain that the subjunctive's ambiguity is not homonymy but polysemy, we are left with the problem of demonstrating the connection between its meanings, and this is scarcely different from the original problem of reconciling its uses. I will not argue that the subjunctive is not ambiguous, for I think that whether it is or not depends only on what we choose to regard as ambiguity. I will try to show, however, that the subjunctive conveys one consistent element of meaning in all its uses (or it did, at least, before its obsolescence). I regard this element of meaning as its semantic content, and I would argue that if we wish to regard the subjunctive as polysemous, its different senses are best explained by reference to pragmatic, and not semantic meaning.

2.2 MODALITY AND MODAL FORMS

Traditional grammars usually define mood by saying such things as that it expresses the mental attitude of the speaker or that it signifies manner of predication or manner of representation.[6] Such differences in definition do not reflect significant differences in the way that mood is conceived, but are merely different ways of saying essentially the same thing. The manner in which the verb is predicated of its subject determines the manner in which the state of affairs indicated by that predication is represented, so the second two definitions are equivalent. The first is not quite equivalent to the other two. Although the speaker will often choose a manner of representation which reflects his attitude toward the situation, the choice may also reflect someone else's attitude, so to define mood as speaker's attitude is too restrictive. To define mood as manner of representation is not restrictive in this way and is quite satisfactory in my view. But traditional grammars do not clarify the notion 'manner of representation'. Instead they give examples of how moods function semantically, showing how one mood expresses command and another statement or how one expresses thoughts and another facts. In order to distinguish the subjunctive from the indicative, I will offer an interpretation of the key term, 'manner of representation'.

The interpretation begins with a hypothesis that there are two fundamental manners of representation. It is a philosophical hypothesis about all kinds of representation, linguistic or otherwise. It is reminiscent of a distinction that philosophers, past and present, have drawn between practical and theoretical reasoning. Particularly, it is reminiscent of the distinction that the philosophical grammarian James Harris draws between two fundamental "powers of the soul". He calls these powers "perception" and "volition", explaining that he intends the terms in an extended sense. By "powers of perception" he means "the senses and the intellect". By "powers of volition" he means "not only the will, but the several passions and appetites", and these include "all that moves to action". Harris goes on to claim that "all speech is a publication of these powers", and, therefore, that "every sentence will be either a sentence of assertion or a sentence of volition". (See Harris 1751: 13-17.)

Very similar distinctions are made more recently by G. E. M. Anscombe and by John Searle. Anscombe distinguishes between two separate kinds of lists, exemplified by a shopper's list, according to which a man selects items in a grocery store, and a detective's list, which another person makes by recording everything the shopper puts into his basket. Anscombe observes that two kinds of mistakes can occur: in the first case, "if the list and the things that the man actually buys do not agree ... , then the mistake is not in the list but in the man's performance"; but in the other case, "if the detective's record and what the man actually buys do not agree, then the mistake is in the record". (See Anscombe 1957: 56.) The lists reflect a fundamental difference in their manner of representation. Searle describes this as a difference between the way in which the words are intended to match the world: when mistakes are made, the shopper fails to get the world to match the words, and the detective fails to get the words to match the world. A correspondence between words and world can be intended in either of two ways. (See Searle 1972: 346-347.)

Words on lists are of course representations, and what Searle says about the kinds of match between words and world holds equally well for non-linguistic representations. Consider, for example, an architect's sketch of a house he plans to build. He intends for the world to match the sketch, which is his 'blueprint'. Now consider an artist's sketch of that house after it is built. He intends for the sketch, which is his 'record', to match the world. The sketches may look exactly alike, but they differ in their manner of representation. If the same person had occasion to draw both kinds of sketches, he might choose to do 'blueprints' on blue paper and 'records' on yellow paper, to help keep orderly files. The colors would then serve to signify manner of representation. Modal forms are the linguistic analogue of this color-coding, and modality is just a linguistic term for manner of representation. Manner of representation is the relation (of which there are two kinds) between a representation and what is represented. The semantic function of modal forms is to signify, and usually also to qualify, one of the two basic modalities. Moods, as systems of inflection on verbs, are a subclass of the larger class of modal forms. Before turning to the moods, I will briefly examine some non-inflectional modal forms, auxiliaries, adjectives, and adverbs, for these help to confirm the hypothesis that there arc two separate kinds of modality.

2.3 MODAL AUXILIARIES AND OTHER MODALS

The ambiguity between the root and epistemic senses of the modal auxiliaries is an ambiguity between these two kinds of modality. In the root sense, *can* means ability, *may* permission, *must* obligation, *shall* determination, and *will* intention. In the root sense, they refer to what are powers of volition in Harris's terminology: they are antecedents of action. (Ability should be included as a 'power of volition' because, although it may not 'move to action', it is a requisite of action.) In the epistemic sense, *can* and *may* mean theoretical possibility, *must* means theoretical necessity, and *shall* and *will* mean futurity. As the term 'epistemic' suggests, in this sense they refer to powers of perception in Harris's terminology: they involve the exercise of the senses or the intellect. In Searle's terminology, to represent a situation as within someone's ability, as permitted to someone, as an obligation of someone, as determined to be brought about by someone, or as intended by someone is in each case to make a representation for the world to match. The root modals have the modality in common. They differ semantically in the qualifications they add beyond specifying a particular modality. Likewise, to represent a situation as theoretically possible, theoretically necessary, or belonging to the future is to make a representation which matches the world. The epistemic modals have the modality in common and differ in the qualifications they add beyond it.

The semantics of modal auxiliaries is complicated by the fact that they can serve not only to attribute properties to the subject of a sentence but also, like moods, to determine the illocutionary potential of a sentence. (Illocutionary potential is the range of illocutionary forces that a sentence can have when uttered, illocutionary force is the communicative purpose with which a sentence is used to perform a speech act, and a speech act is an act of using language for doing such things as giving orders, making promises, and reporting information.) Julian Boyd and J. P. Thorne show that in certain uses in independent clauses, the auxiliaries can be analyzed as modifying one or another of two primary speech acts, statements and imperatives. *May*, for instance, in the sentence *He may go*, determines illocutionary potential if the sentence means 'I permit him to go' (but not if it means 'He has permission to go'). 'I permit' can be analyzed as 'I do not forbid', and 'I forbid', as 'I command... not'. In this way *may* can be taken as a modification of an imperative. By contrast, *may* can be taken as a modification of a statement if *He may go* means 'I do not deny that he goes', for 'I deny' can be analyzed as 'I state... not'. Since the communicative purpose of statements is to get words to match the world, and the communicative purpose of imperatives is to get the world to match words, the auxiliaries are still ambiguous between two kinds of modality, whether or not they determine illocutionary potential. (See Boyd and Thorne 1969.)

The modal adjective *possible*, as Ian Hacking points out, exhibits an ambiguity comparable to the ambiguity in the modal auxiliaries. Hacking notes that there are two kinds of possibility and that these are not identical: one does not entail the other. Giving an example, he says, "It may be possible for the judge to give the woman a suspended sentence, but it is not possible that he will; he is notoriously mean and will certainly send her to jail" (Hacking 1975: 323). If we say, "It is possible for the judge to do it," meaning he has the legal authority to do it, *possible* specifies the same modality as *can* and *may* in the root sense. This kind of possibility is potential, and 'potential' is semantically similar to 'ability' and 'permission', being somewhat more general and often implying both. If we say, "It is possible that the judge will do it," meaning there is some chance of his doing it, *possible* specifies the same modality as *can* and *may* in the epistemic sense, for this kind of possibility is theoretical possibility. The words *necessary* and *necessarily* show that there are two kinds of necessity, just as there are two kinds of possibility. If we say, "It is necessary for him to do that," *necessary* specifies the same modality as *must* in the root sense, and if we say, "That is necessarily the case," *necessarily* specifies the same modality as *must* in the epistemic sense.

2.4 MOODS

The ambiguity of the modal auxiliaries, which is reflected in words denoting possibility and necessity, supports the hypothesis that there are two separate manners of representation. Moods, like the auxiliaries and some other words, signify manners of representation. They are not ambiguous, however; they signify one modality or the other. They are also comparatively simple semantically, for they signify very little beyond a basic modality. The imperative and subjunctive signify Harris's volitions, that is, the blueprint, or world-to-match-words modality, and the indicative signifies Harris's perceptions, the record, or words-to-match-world modality. The imperative is semantically distinct from the subjunctive only in two respects: first, its distribution is more limited than the subjunctive's (recall that I ignore the subjunctive's obsolescence), as it is restricted to the second person, present tense, and to independent clauses, and second, it refers the bringing about of the state of affairs represented in the clause in which it occurs to the subject of that clause. The subjunctive is not restricted syntactically in the way that the imperative is, nor does it refer the bringing about of the state of affairs to anyone in particular. The indicative is like the subjunctive in lacking the kinds of added information that the imperative conveys. Together the three moods divide the semantic domain of modality in conformity with the hypothesis that there are two basic manners of representation.

For convenience I will refer to the two manners of representation as 'practical' and 'theoretical', from the Greek words meaning 'doing' and 'viewing'.[7] The new terms will prove less awkward than the terms I have been using and more inclusive than terms that have been used previously to describe modal ambiguity. In this terminology, representations like blueprints or shoppers' lists are practical and those like records or detectives' lists are theoretical. The practical modality corresponds to Harris's volitions. It is the modality of the modal auxiliaries in the root sense and of *possible* and *necessary* with *for . . . to* complements. The theoretical modality corresponds to Harris's perceptions. It is the modality of the modal auxiliaries in the epistemic sense, of *possible* with *that*-clause complements, and of *necessarily*. Since I regard modality as the relation between words and world, the best way to paraphrase my terms would be to call the practical modality the world-to-match-words modality, and the theoretical modality the words-to-match-world modality. I will now try to establish that the subjunctive mood signifies no more nor less than the practical modality. Signifying practical modality, the subjunctive is semantically distinct from the indicative, which signifies theoretical modality. The subjunctive is distinct from the imperative, which also signifies practical modality, in not conveying any additional information. If we take the semantic content of the subjunctive to be limited to the practical modality, we will be able to account for its apparently different meanings in different uses.

2.5 USES OF THE PRESENT SUBJUNCTIVE

Analyzing the meanings of moods in particular uses involves sorting out and finding sources for different kinds of information. The word 'meaning' is a vague, pretheoretical term. Traditional studies describing the meanings of the moods have assigned nearly all information about the manner in which a clause represents a state of affairs to the mood of the main verb. But much of the information about manner of representation is qualifying information coming not from the mood but from the particular use, coming, that is, from other forms in the sentence or from the context in which the sentence typically or actually occurs. Assigning too much information to the mood makes reconciling its uses impossible. By assuming that the subjunctive conveys the very limited information that manner of representation is practical, we avoid this problem. What remains to show is how the information conveyed by the subjunctive combines with information from other sources to produce the effects observable in particular uses. To do this, we must distinguish the signification of a form, information which the form itself conveys, from the implications of a form, information deducible from the form as it occurs in context. Analysis will show that meanings which grammarians have traditionally assigned to the moods, meanings such as 'statement', 'fact', 'certain', 'actual', or 'real' for the indicative and 'wish', 'thought', 'uncertain', 'potential', or 'unreal' for the subjunctive, are implications which derive automatically from the signification of a mood and the qualifying information in typical contexts.[8] Being implications, no single one of these meanings always occurs with a given mood, and grammarians assuming any one of them as the mood's basic meaning (signification) have therefore been unable to provide a unified account of the mood's uses.

Below I analyze the present subjunctive in three syntactic environments, independent clauses, noun clauses, and adverb clauses. Important sources of qualifying information I consider in analyzing particular uses are the syntactic environment itself, the communicative purpose of the clause, and the point of view from which a state of affairs is represented. Syntactic environment has an effect in determining how information about manner of representation may be qualified. Information conveyed by moods in independent clauses, clauses which are complete and available for use in performing speech acts, is qualified by requirements for performing speech acts and by context of utterance. Information conveyed by moods in dependent clauses, clauses which are parts of larger units, is qualified by the matrix in which the clause is embedded. The communicative purpose of the clause in which a mood occurs has an effect, because mood is an obligatory category. The speaker must choose one mood or another for every clause, whether the manner of representation signified by that mood is fully appropriate to the purpose of the clause or not. Point of view has an effect on choice of mood, for a mood, signifying primarily or exclusively an intended relation between words and world, can reflect either the point of view of the speaker or that of someone identified in the context of utterance or in a matrix sentence, and it can reflect the point of view of the speaker either at the time of speaking or at some other time determined by context. Since one mood may be appropriate from one point of view, but a different mood may be appropriate from another, the point of view from which a state of affairs is represented may determine which mood is used. Keeping these sources of qualifying information in mind, I will show how the subjunctive, in context, produces such meanings as 'wish' as opposed to 'statement' or 'command', and 'thought' or 'unreal' as opposed to 'fact' or 'real', meanings which have often been considered the semantic content of the mood itself.

2.5.1 INDEPENDENT CLAUSES

> *So be it*
> *God bless you*
> *Be this sweet Helen's knell*
> *Enter Hamlet reading a book*

To analyze the meanings that moods acquire in independent clauses, we will need to clarify the traditional notion of sentence type, and to do the latter we will need to clarify the notoriously slippery notion of a sentence. Although an 'independent clause' is traditionally defined as a clause which makes a sentence when standing alone, the results of generative grammar suggest that it will be easier to define 'sentence' in terms of 'independent clause' (see Chomsky 1957 and 1965). A 'clause', traditionally defined as a group of related words having a subject and a predicate, can be identified on formal grounds. (In Indo-European languages, a clause is a group of related words with a finite verb and with a substantive, sometimes optional, in the nominative or vocative case.) An 'independent clause' is a clause not embedded as a constituent of another clause. The generative rule embodying the traditional definition of a clause is S → NP + VP (a clause is composed of a subject noun phrase and a predicate verb phrase). An S-node represents an independent clause if it is not immediately dominated by any node except possibly another S-node (an independent clause may be conjoined, but not subjoined, to another clause). While the notion 'independent clause' can be adequately defined on syntactic grounds within a formal theory of syntax such as generative grammar provides, the notions 'sentence' and 'sentence type' cannot. The concepts that 'sentence types' express can be formalized with symbols like IMP (imperative) and Q (interrogative), but the concepts themselves require analysis.

A 'sentence', traditionally defined, expresses a complete thought, but what is a complete thought? A theory of use, such as speech act theory, can elucidate this notion of 'sentence'. In speech act theory, a 'sentence' is definable as a single independent clause or two or more independent clauses conjoined which can be used to perform a speech act, a 'speech act' being an act of communicating with a linguistic representation. 'Sentence types' enumerate very general kinds of speech acts that independent clauses can be used to perform. The traditional types, declarative, imperative, and interrogative, categorize independent clauses according to their potential illocutionary force (communicative purpose), and illocutionary force is a pragmatic aspect of meaning. The terms 'declarative', 'imperative', and 'interrogative' do not refer to semantic information conveyed by formal elements of sentences, but rather to the illocutionary potential of moods in independent clauses.

The formal element marking the end of a sentence, rising or falling intonation with full pause (or end punctuation in writing), conveys the semantic information that an utterance (speech act) is complete and whether it is a *yes-no* question. Mood signifies the intended relation between words and world, and context shows who intends the relation (usually the speaker). Consider the sentence,

You are early.

We take this sentence, when actually spoken, as declarative (we infer its illocutionary force) by taking it as complete, not a *yes-no* question, and as a representation which the speaker intends to match the world.

Formal and contextual features combine, in the absence of any additional complicating contextual features, to imply that the person speaking the sentence is making a statement, and a 'declarative sentence' is just an independent clause which the speaker can use to make a statement.

Next consider the imperative sentence,

Be early.

Intonation with full pause conveys the same information as in the declarative sentence. Mood (the inflection on the verb, which is also called 'imperative') signifies that someone (the speaker unless otherwise indicated) intends the world to match the representation. The imperative's further syntactic and semantic restrictions (subcategorization and selection restrictions) that limit it to independent clauses (or subordinate clauses in sentences which quote independent clauses verbatim) require it to be present tense and second person and require its subject to be either deleted or pronounced with special, 'vocative' intonation, deletion or intonation showing that the second person subject is being addressed. The imperative also specifies a relation between the subject of the clause and the state of affairs represented by referring the bringing about of the state of affairs to the subject. The mood's signification, including syntactic and semantic restrictions, will imply that the speaker uttering a complete sentence which is not a *yes-no* question is giving a command to the hearer, and an 'imperative sentence' is just an independent clause which the speaker can use to give a command.

Now consider the two interrogative sentences,

Are you early?

Be early?

Intonation and full pause show in each case that the utterance is complete, and rising intonation shows that the utterance is a *yes-no* question. Rising intonation adds qualifying information to the information conveyed by the moods, by conveying that the speaker does not intend the words to match the world nor the world to match the words, but wants the hearer to commit himself to one relation or the other. In the absence of such qualifying information, we infer that the speaker intends the relation signified by mood. As with the declarative sentence *You are early* and the imperative sentence *Be early*, formal and contextual features combine to imply that the speaker is asking a question with *Are you early?* or *Be early?,* and an 'interrogative sentence' is just an independent clause which the speaker can use to ask a question.

Employing a formal notation, we can show schematically how the information conveyed by moods combines with information from other sources. We symbolize the propositional content of a clause in the way that is customary in logic, and we symbolize the manner of representation that modal forms signify, which according to the theory proposed is always either 'practical' or 'theoretical', with the abbreviations 'prac' and 'theor'. The tenses convey information that qualifies modality, and with the abbreviations 'pres' and 'past', we symbolize the temporal concepts they signify. The signification of the present tense is 'not earlier than present time' (present tense is interpreted as meaning 'present time' unless context shows that it means 'future time'), and the signification of the past tense is 'past time'. With the punctuation marks '.' and '?' we symbolize the semantic information conveyed by falling and rising intonation. The semantic information conveyed in the sentences *You are early, Be early, Are you early?,* and *Be early?*[9] is as follows:

.(pres/theor (Early (you)))

.(pres/imperative-prac (Early (you)))

?(pres/theor (Early (you)))

?(pres/imperative-prac (Early (you)))

The slash between the significations of tenses and modals means 'and' and indicates that the tense does not have the modal within its scope and that the modal does not have the tense within its scope. The slash is an abbreviation, and the string,

.(pres/theor (Early (you)))

could be expanded as follows:

.((pres (Early (you))) & (theor (Early (you))))

The notation captures an assumption that the indicative mood signifies only the theoretical modality. The imperative mood, with its special restrictions, signifies more than the practical modality, however, and the residual information is symbolized by the name of the form itself. I attempt to describe residual semantic information beyond basic manner of representation only to the extent that it qualifies manner of representation. I describe this information separately, capitalizing aspects of meaning which recur or vary systematically among forms, such as subcategorization and selection restrictions. With this addition, the schematic description for the sentence *Be early* is as follows:

.(pres/imperative-prac (Early (you)))

> imperative: is limited to INDEPENDENT CLAUSES in which the SUBJECT IS ADDRESSED and signifies that the independent clause represents a state of affairs in the PRACTICAL modality and that the state of affairs is something FOR THE SUBJECT TO BRING ABOUT

Saying that the state of affairs is represented in the practical modality merely repeats what the abbreviation 'prac' already says in the first line of the description, but saying that the state of affairs is for the subject to bring about does not. Information about the relation between the subject and the state of affairs represented in the clause is information beyond basic modality. It is like information about the relation between a predicate and its subject or between a verb and its complements, and the imperative mood is to this extent similar to such verbs as *order, request,* and *advise.* For instance, the sentence *Be early* is semantically very similar to the sentence,

I order you to be early.

We can describe this sentence schematically as follows:

.(pres/theor (Order-prac (I, you, Early (you))))

> order: requires a HUMAN SUBJECT, a HUMAN DIRECT OBJECT, and an INFINITIVE COMPLEMENT and signifies that the infinitive complement represents a state of affairs in the PRACTICAL modality and that the state of affairs is something FOR THE HUMAN DIRECT OBJECT TO BRING ABOUT

> note: The word 'requires' indicates a restriction, but restrictions are not stated fully. Alternative restrictions, as would be needed to account for the use of *order* in *I ordered coffee,* for instance, are not listed.

Comparing the schematic descriptions for *I order you to be early* and *Be early,* we note that the word *order* is an ordinary predicate taking three arguments, two of which tell explicitly who is giving the command and who is receiving the command. The imperative is not an ordinary predicate. Like the other moods, it functions semantically as a special kind of predicate, one which takes as arguments only other predicates with their arguments. The imperative cannot have arguments which refer to persons, as *order* can, but in the absence of additional information, it is assumed that the speaker is giving the command and the hearer receiving it, and so in typical uses *Be early* means the same as *I order you to be early*. This assumption can be canceled however, as in the sentences *"Be early," he said* or *The order was "Be early"* or in the discourse *He said only two things: "The meeting is important. Be early."* In such cases we take the person giving the command, not as 'I', the current speaker, but as some unspecified earlier speaker, and we take the person receiving the command, not as 'you', the current hearer, but as some unspecified earlier hearer.

Another difference is that since *order* is a verb in English, it must be specified for mood when it functions as the predicate of a sentence, and since mood is indicative in *I order you to be early,* the manner of representation for the whole sentence is theoretical. Yet, the verb *order* is a performative verb, in J. L. Austin's sense, and so the sentence typically gives a command as the imperative sentence does (see Austin 1962). 'Performativeness' is a pragmatic aspect of meaning, however, and is cancelable. As Austin himself points out, 'performativeness' is canceled in all but first person, present tense, non-progressive, non-habitual uses. But performativeness is cancelable even for the sentence *I order you to be early* when it meets these conditions. In the following discourse, in which the speaker describes events he is imagining, the sentence does not give a command: the speaker says, "Here's the plan. When you come in I appear to be annoyed. I order you to be early . . . ." In this discourse, the sentence only describes an action, it does not perform one, and there is no reason not to say that the declarative sentence *I order you to be early* always describes an action.[10] None of Austin's insights are lost if we maintain that in the ordinary use of certain verbs, the speaker using the verb performs the action in describing the action. When such verbs are used in the ordinary way, it is strange for the hearer to respond "true" or "false", but this is because he then seems to mistake the primary purpose of the utterance, which is to perform the action, not describe it. If I say to someone "I order you to be early," and he responds, saying "Yes you do, although I have no reason to obey," he has taken my sentence as a description. He has responded, "True. You order me to be early, although I have no reason to obey." Such a response to an imperative sentence would not be merely strange, it would be impossible because imperative sentences do not describe acts of ordering as declarative sentences with the word *order* do.

Point of view, a pragmatic aspect of meaning which qualifies modality, I also treat separately, associating it with the significations of temporal and modal forms in a list below the schematic description of the semantic information conveyed by a clause. In the absence of information to the contrary, both tenses and moods are assumed to reflect the point of view of the speaker at the time of speaking. This information for the sentence *You are early* can be listed as follows:

.(pres/theor (Early (you)))

    pres – speaker
    theor – speaker

The new lines of the description mean that from the speaker's current point of view, the time of the state of affairs is not earlier than present and that from the speaker's current point of view, the state of affairs is something which the words match. Combined semantic and pragmatic information show that the simple sentence *You are early* makes a statement. The speaker uses the independent clause to do no more nor less than represent the world as it is at the time of speaking, and this is what it means to make a statement about a present state of affairs.

Combined semantic and pragmatic information for the sentence *Be early* is as follows:

.(pres/imperative-prac (Early (you)))

    pres – speaker
    prac – speaker and addressee: for the addressee to bring about

From the speaker's current point of view, the state of affairs 'your being early' is something to be brought about. From the subject's point of view, the state of affairs 'your being early' is also something to be brought about, because the imperative refers the state of affairs to the subject of the clause, the addressee. Combined semantic and pragmatic information show that the simple sentence *Be early* gives a command.

The speaker typically uses the clause to get the hearer to bring about the state of affairs represented, and this is what it means to give a command.

Pragmatic information about point of view will change with context. In contexts in which it is clear that the speaker is not using independent clauses to perform speech acts, as when he is speaking for someone else, or in verbatim reports, in which clauses seem to assume a status midway between independent and dependent, the point of view is not the speaker's. Consider the complex sentence,

"You are early," the man said.

The clause in quotation marks is qualified to show that the speaker is not using it to make a statement. It is technically a subordinate clause, functioning as the direct object of *said*. The clause is pronounced with half-falling intonation and half-pause, and these prosodic features show that the subject of the main clause, the original speaker, has used the clause to make a statement. Using quotation marks around the period to symbolize the information conveyed by half-falling intonation, we can describe semantic information for the sentence schematically as follows:

.(past/theor$_1$ (Say (man, ". "(pres/theor$_2$ (Early (you)))))))

Combined semantic and pragmatic information for the subordinate clause in question is as follows:

pres/theor$_2$ (Early (you))

> pres - one who says (man): man's time of speaking
> theor$_2$ - one who says (man)

Context shows that in the reported sentence, the present tense reflects the point of view of the original speaker, the subject of the main clause, as does the indicative mood. As a similar case, consider the sentence,

The man's advice was "Be early."

Semantic and pragmatic information for the subordinate clause is as follows:

pres/imperative-prac (Early (you))

    pres - one who advises (man): man's time of speaking
    prac - one who advises (man) and addressee (unspecified)

Beyond the usual meanings in ordinary uses, a mood may acquire apparently different meanings in independent clauses because specific contexts provide a great deal of further qualifying information about manner of representation. Consider again the imperative in independent clauses. Typically it means command, but we cannot say that the mood itself signifies command. What it does signify is that the speaker intends for a state of affairs to match a sentence (practical modality) and that the sentence is a directive (in a broad sense) for the hearer to bring about the situation referred to. The signification of the imperative will imply command in many contexts—if, for instance, the speaker is of higher social status than the hearer and sincerely wants the situation to be brought about. If the speaker is of lower status, the imperative means request, and if the speaker does not care whether the situation is brought about, as in instructions of the form "Do this to get that," then the imperative means prescription (in a weak sense). The meaning 'command' in simple sentences, we see, results in large part from specific pragmatic information.

The indicative in simple declarative sentences typically means statement, but again we cannot call this the mood's signification. The mood does no more than set up a particular kind of relation between a clause and a state of affairs. It does not even imply that this relation (words matching world) actually holds; rather, it is falling intonation and an absence of qualifying information that does this. In interrogative sentences the indicative does not mean statement, for rising intonation qualifies the information conveyed by the mood, showing that the speaker does not know whether the relation holds. The meaning 'statement', we see, arises partly from the mood and partly from falling intonation, and 'statement' still only describes a typical meaning of the indicative in declarative sentences. With adjustments in context, the indicative in declarative sentences can mean supposition, guess, belief, or the like, just as the imperative can mean things other than command.

The meanings 'command' for the imperative and 'statement' for the indicative arise largely from the pragmatic information supplied by the context of independent clauses. These meanings typically arise in independent clauses, but only because such clauses have illocutionary potential. In dependent clauses, which do not express 'complete thoughts' and lack illocutionary potential, the indicative cannot mean statement. In order to reconcile the indicative's uses in simple declarative sentences, simple interrogative sentences, and dependent clauses, we must extract its semantic content from the meanings it acquires in such particular uses.

The subjunctive is no different from the imperative or the indicative in the way it gets its meaning in context. In independent clauses, it typically means wish, which, like 'command' and 'statement', is the name of an illocutionary force. The meaning 'wish' in non-interrogative sentences arises in the following way. The mood signifies that the state of affairs represented is seen in light of action. The subjunctive, not referring to any specific antecedent of action and not giving a directive to the hearer, does no more than represent the state of affairs as something to be brought about. The most general case of a state of affairs represented as to be brought about, the case in which the fewest restrictions are placed on the antecedents of action, is one in which the state of affairs is desirable or obligatory, there is potential for its coming into being, and, if it is a state of affairs over which the speaker has control, is willed. Such a state of affairs is a wish whose fulfilment is possible, and so in the absence of further qualifying information, the subjunctive will imply 'wish'. Consider the sentence,

God bless you.

Typically this sentence expresses wish. Semantic and pragmatic information combine as follows:

.(pres/prac (Bless (God, you)))

pres - speaker
prac - speaker

Though restricted to fossilized expressions in the modern language, this use of the present subjunctive is fully productive in earlier English. Examples from earlier English follow:

Geweorðe me æfter þinum worde. (p. 796)
'Let it be with me according to your word.'

Be this sweet Helen's knell. (p. 797)

As in the fossilized modern example, the subjunctive in these three sentences implies 'wish'.

Yet, the meaning 'wish' is cancelable, just as 'command' and 'statement' are. The sentence *So be it* might express wish, but if the situation it refers to has already come about, it expresses condonement, approval, or resignation. The stage direction *Enter Hamlet reading a book* does not express wish.[12] The meaning of the subjunctive is prescription in this context, much like the meaning of the imperative in instructions. In all these contexts, however, the subjunctive signifies practical modality, with the world intended to match the words. This is probably obvious in the examples of wish and prescription, but perhaps less so in the case of condonement. It is important to keep in mind though that the moods only signify one of two possible relations between words and world: by themselves moods imply nothing about actuality. The same would be true of our color-coding in non-linguistic representation. An architect's sketch is still a 'blueprint' after the house is built, and an artist's sketch is still a 'record' after the house is destroyed. Our blue and our yellow paper would retain their functions whether what was drawn on them existed or not.

2.5.2 NOUN CLAUSES

They insist that it be so
I hope he be in love
Y trowe thy knyfe be gode y-nogh
he segð, þæt he si Crist cyning
Now aske of me what it be

Reconciling the subjunctive's current use in noun clauses with its use in independent clauses is not difficult. Noun clauses are dependent, and so have no illocutionary potential. If we abstract from the illocutionary features of the subjunctive in independent clauses, we have its meaning in object clauses. Since the meanings it has in independent clauses are 'wish', 'condonement', 'prescription', and the like, we must abstract from these. 'Wish', 'condonement', and 'prescription' are all either illocutionary acts or psychological attitudes associated with such acts, and these acts and attitudes have in common that they require reference to situations which must be represented in the practical manner. The difference between the subjunctive in the independent clause of the simple sentence *So be it* and in the dependent clause of the complex sentence *They insist that it be so* is that qualifying information supplied for the independent clause by the context of utterance is supplied for the dependent clause by the main verb of the sentence together with its subject. The similarity is that the subjunctive in both the independent and dependent clauses signifies that the situation, 'its being so', is a volition in the extended sense. It is something to be brought about and not something to be apprehended by the senses or intellect.

Because the subjunctive in noun clauses is not affected by illocutionary features, such clauses provide a better environment than independent clauses for determining the semantic information it conveys. We are less apt to associate incidental, non-inherent features of meaning with the mood itself. We note that a clause like *that it be so* is compatible with such qualifying expressions as *they insist, they request, they demand, it is their desire, it is their wish,* and so forth, but because it is compatible with all, it cannot itself signify what any particular one signifies. We also note that a qualifying expression like *they insist,* the word *insist* being mainly an intensifier, allows object clauses in either the subjunctive or the indicative, and so provides an ideal test-frame for comparing the meanings of the two moods. Consider the difference between the two sentences,

They insist that it be so.

They insist that it is so.

The difference is just that the representation of the situation, 'its being so', purportedly is to be matched by the world in the first, but purportedly matches the world in the second. The situation is something to be brought about in the first, something to be perceived in the second.

With the notation we have used to describe independent clauses, we can describe semantic and pragmatic information for forms which signify or qualify the modality of noun clauses. Taking 'its being so' as an unanalyzable proposition, we describe semantic information for the two sentences above as follows:

.(pres_1/theor (Insist (they, pres_2/prac (So))))

.(pres_1/theor_1 (Insist (they, pres_2/theor_2 (So))))

Combined semantic and pragmatic information for the noun clauses *it be so* and *it is so* is as follows:

pres_2/prac (So)

    pres_2 - ones who insist (they) and speaker
    prac - ones who insist (they)

pres$_2$/theor$_2$ (So)

> pres$_2$ - ones who insist (they) and speaker
> theor$_2$ - ones who insist (they)

Modality is the same as in the independent clauses *So be it* and *It is so,* but pragmatic information about point of view is supplied by the matrix clause, not the context of utterance.

The verb *insist* does not signify modality but qualifies modality, showing that its subject is strongly committed to the view that the relation between words and world signified by the modal form in its noun clause complement holds. Information about modality comes solely from the moods, as *insist* places no restrictions on the kinds of modal forms that can occur in its complement. In not selecting one mood or the other, the verb *insist* differs from the verb *request,* as it occurs in the sentence,

> They request that it be so.

We describe semantic information for this sentence as follows:

> .(pres$_1$/theor (Request-prac$_1$ (they, pres$_2$/prac$_2$ (So))))

Differences between *insist* and *request* are brought out in the following lexical descriptions:

> insist: requires a HUMAN SUBJECT and a NOUN CLAUSE DIRECT OBJECT and signifies STRONG COMMITMENT

> request: requires a HUMAN SUBJECT and a NOUN CLAUSE DIRECT OBJECT and signifies that the noun clause represents a state of affairs in the PRACTICAL modality and that the state of affairs is something FOR SOMEONE TO BRING ABOUT

Since the verb *request* both signifies practical modality and places a selection restriction on the modality of the noun clause complement, the modality signified by the subjunctive mood is redundant. In the sentence *They request us to do it* modality in the complement is clearly practical, although the infinitive does not signify modality. Semantic information for the sentence is as follows (compare the description for *I order you to be early,* Section 2.5.1):

.(pres/theor (Request-prac (they, us, Do (we, it))))

request: requires a HUMAN SUBJECT, a HUMAN DIRECT OB-
JECT, and an INFINITIVE COMPLEMENT and signifies that
the infinitive complement represents a state of affairs in the
PRACTICAL modality and that the state of affairs is something
FOR THE HUMAN DIRECT OBJECT TO BRING ABOUT

Pragmatic information about point of view for the two sentences with
request, as for the sentences with *insist,* comes from the matrix clause.

Some of the subjunctive's earlier uses in noun clauses are more difficult than its current uses to explain. The following sentences exemplify
the subjunctive after verbs of hoping and believing:

I hope he be in love. (p. 850)

Y trowe thy knyfe be gode y-nogh. (p. 851)
'I believe your knife be good enough.'

Such uses were once fairly common, even as recently as Early Modern
English. Somewhat less common but still frequent, especially in Old
and Middle English, are uses after verbs of saying and asking (indirect
discourse). Visser cites the sentences,

he segð, þæt he si Crist cyning. (p. 854)
'he says that he be Christ king.'

Now aske of me what it be. (p. 857)

Know of the duke, if his last purpose hold. (p. 857)

Uses such as these five, like the subjunctive's use in conditional
clauses, are difficult to explain because both subjunctive and indicative
occur in such contexts without apparent difference in meaning, and
there has been variation between moods throughout the history of the
language (with the subjunctive becoming less and less frequent). Yet
we can explain the variation while maintaining that the subjunctive signifies practical modality. To do so we must note the qualifying effects
of the main clauses which embed the clauses containing the moods.

In the five uses at hand, we can find reasons for using either mood
and thus explain the variation. One reason for using the subjunctive in
the complement of emotion verbs like *hope* and *fear* is that such verbs

indicate the desirability or undesirability of the state of affairs represented in the complement. If one hopes for a state of affairs, one wishes for it, and if the state of affairs is a future state of affairs, one might also request it, and so the subjunctive is appropriate for the same reason that it is appropriate in independent clauses (typically expressing wish) and in dependent clauses after verbs of requesting. Another reason for using the subjunctive with *hope* and *fear* is that there may be some doubt about the actuality of the state of affairs represented in the complement, and if the subject of the verb is first person, there is always doubt. This makes the subjunctive appropriate, because it cannot imply that words match world. On the other hand, there are reasons for using the indicative with these verbs. The emotions involved may have existing or previously existing states of affairs as their objects and therefore not be antecedents of action. Since existing and previously existing states of affairs can be perceived, they are appropriately represented by the indicative. Since these emotions may involve both belief (or expectation) and desirability, their objects may appropriately be represented either as volitions or perceptions, in the practical manner or the theoretical.[13] A semantic description of *hope* must reflect that this verb expresses both desirability and belief. Semantic information for the sentence *I hope he be in love* is as follows:

.(pres$_1$/theor$_1$ (Hope-prac$_1$/theor$_2$ (I, pres$_2$/prac$_2$ (Love (he)))))

> hope: requires a HUMAN SUBJECT and a NOUN CLAUSE DIRECT OBJECT and signifies that the noun clause represents a state of affairs that the subject regards as DESIRABLE and as THEORETICALLY POSSIBLE

Pragmatic information for the subordinate clause is as follows:

> pres$_2$ - one who hopes (I)
> prac$_2$ - one who hopes (I)

The verb *hope* has undergone a change since Early Modern English and now requires its complement to represent a state of affairs in the theoretical modality. Semantic information for the present-day sentence *I hope he is in love* is as follows:

.(pres$_1$/theor$_1$ (Hope-prac/theor$_2$ (I, pres$_2$/theor$_3$ (Love (he)))))

> hope: requires a HUMAN SUBJECT and a NOUN CLAUSE DI-

RECT OBJECT in the INDICATIVE mood and signifies that the
noun clause represents a state of affairs that the subject regards
as DESIRABLE and as THEORETICALLY POSSIBLE

Pragmatic information for the subordinate clause is as follows:

$pres_2$ - one who hopes (I)
$theor_3$ - one who hopes (I)

Since the verb itself signifies both desirability and theoretical possibility and hence both manners of representation, the Early Modern English sentence and the present-day one appear to mean the same thing
despite a difference in mood.

Verbs expressing belief are similar in important respects to verbs expressing emotions like hope and fear. In expressing hope or fear, one
might have a belief about the state of affairs represented, and converse-
ly, in expressing belief, one might have an emotional attitude toward
the state of affairs represented. The compatibility and frequent association of hope or fear with belief makes the same manner of representation appropriate. Also, with verbs of believing, as with verbs of
hoping and fearing, there is doubt about actuality, so the subjunctive is
appropriate for this reason too. Verbs of saying and asking are in many
ways similar to verbs of believing. To say that or ask whether a state of
affairs exists involves beliefs about the state of affairs, and so choice of
mood in the complements of verbs referring to these actions involves
the same concerns as choice of mood in verbs of believing.

The question of actuality and mood is important for all these verbs,
verbs of hoping, fearing, believing, saying, and asking, because with
second or third person subjects we can distinguish two points of view
toward the state of affairs represented in the complement, that of the
subject of the verb and that of the speaker. This creates a potential for a
motivated choice between moods. Consider the complement of *believe*
in the sentence,

He believes it to be so.

The verb of the complement, being an infinitive, does not signify a modality. If one wished to represent the state of affairs in a full clause,
one would have to choose a mood, as mood is an obligatory category of
finite verbs. As one is trying neither to get the words to match the
world nor to get the world to match the words, the choice is not as
straightforward as it is in independent clauses. One might speak the

sentence knowing that the subject is quite certain in his belief, and yet one might be very doubtful oneself or know that the belief is false. On the other hand, one might speak the sentence knowing that the subject is somewhat doubtful, and yet one might be quite certain oneself. By choosing one mood or the other, one might conceivably distinguish one's own attitude from the subject's.

Since in earlier English verbs like *believe* allow either mood, one can say either of the two sentences,

He believes that it be so.

He believes that it is so.

Since one must say one or the other, one might reasonably try to put the choice to some effect. Choosing the subjunctive, one might show that one does not assume a correspondence between words and world, even if the subject regards the state of affairs as probable or certain. The subjunctive can show this because it cannot be interpreted as committing the speaker to such a correspondence. Using the subjunctive and saying "He believes that it be so, but it isn't," one avoids any chance of conflict or confusion which could arise from the two separate points of view. One might not wish to show that one does not assume a correspondence between words and world, however, and so have no reason to choose the subjunctive, and if one does assume a correspondence, one has reason to choose the indicative. Using the indicative and saying "He believes that it is so, and it is so," one can indicate a single attitude despite separate points of view. Since the indicative can commit the speaker to a correspondence between words and world, someone assuming such a correspondence might prefer it over the subjunctive.

We can describe semantic and pragmatic information for the sentence *He believes that it be so* as follows:

.($\text{pres}_1/\text{theor}_1$ (Believe-theor_2 (he, $\text{pres}_2/\text{prac}$ (So))))

believe: requires a HUMAN SUBJECT and a NOUN CLAUSE DIRECT OBJECT and signifies that the noun clause represents a state of affairs in the THEORETICAL modality and that the subject regards the state of affairs as ACTUAL OR PROBABLE

pres_1 - speaker
theor_1 - speaker

theor$_2$ - one who believes (he)
pres$_2$ - one who believes (he) and speaker
prac - speaker and possibly one who believes

Since the verb *believe* does not signify practical modality, the subjunctive in the noun clause may reflect the speaker's point of view. The verb itself signifies that the subject regards the state of affairs as something to be perceived. The corresponding sentence with the indicative, *He believes that it is so,* we can describe as follows:

.(pres$_1$/theor$_1$ (Believe-theor$_2$ (he, pres$_2$/theor$_3$ (So))))

pres$_1$ - speaker
theor$_1$ - speaker
theor$_2$ - one who believes
pres$_2$ - one who believes and speaker
theor$_3$ - one who believes (redundant with theor$_2$) and possibly speaker

On this reading, the modality signified by the indicative may be purely redundant. But if usage is such that a subjunctive in the noun clause consistently reflects the point of view of the speaker, differentiating his point of view from the subject's, then an indicative in the noun clause may also reflect the point of view of the speaker, showing that speaker and subject take the same point of view.

Grammarians of both English and other languages that use a subjunctive or optative mood in such constructions have said that the subjunctive or optative is employed to distinguish points of view, and especially to indicate the speaker's uncertainty. They have also said that the indicative is employed to show more certainty. Granting that speakers do attempt to put the choice to some effect, these statements are quite plausible. However, except that grammarians who wrote when the subjunctive was still used in these constructions have made such statements, there is little evidence that choice of mood was ever carefully and systematically motivated in English. Since choice of mood is so inconsistent, I incline to think that speakers often preferred one mood or the other rather arbitrarily, allowing variation, or else they chose one mood with one verb, and the other mood with another (say, the subjunctive with *hope,* the indicative with *believe*), again allowing variation. In any case, variation can occur because the semantic information conveyed by the verb of the main clause is sufficient to make the choice of mood largely irrelevant.

Just as verbs like *require* and *prefer* themselves signify practical modality and so make a subjunctive in their complements redundant, so verbs like *believe* and *know* signify theoretical modality. No important semantic information is lost in substituting complements which do not contain modals. Consider the two sentences with infinitive complements,

> They require it to be so.

> They believe it to be so.

These sentences are just as clear as the corresponding sentences with noun clause complements,

> They require that it be so.

> They believe that it is so.

Because the main verbs show modality from the subject's point of view, the speaker can choose a modality that conforms with this point of view (as in modern usage) or departs from it (as was possible in earlier usage) without confusing the subject's manner of representation. This option creates an opportunity for the speaker to reflect his own point of view in the complement. Someone regarding someone else's belief as something potential or desirable might then say *They believe that it be so.* Someone regarding someone else's requirement as something actual might say *They require that it is so,* and in fact, examples of the indicative with verbs expressing volition have occurred since Old English times.[14] Speakers probably took advantage of the option in moods, but it is difficult to ascertain earlier patterns of usage, and there is no current pattern of distinguishing points of view. Rather, verbs have come to select only one mood or the other or to require infinitive complements.

Emotion verbs like *hope* and *fear* present an additional difficulty because they are modally complex. They signify both modalities, because they represent a state of affairs both as desirable (or undesirable) and as theoretically possible. The object of the emotion is therefore represented both in light of action and in light of perception. There is no reason why the two modalities should not combine in some words, for to view a state of affairs both as to be brought about and as to be perceived is not inconsistent. We have seen how a single state of affairs can be regarded in one manner from the speaker's point of view and in the other from the subject's and how this complicates the choice of mood in the complements of verbs of believing and saying; the same is true for verbs of hoping and fearing, but with these the subject's point of view is itself complicated by the nature of the emotion. That the indicative has prevailed with these verbs at the expense of the subjunctive is in keeping with the trend of decline in the subjunctive. The result has been that the subjunctive with *hope* and *fear* is now unidiomatic, although it would not be semantically inappropriate.

2.5.3 ADVERB CLAUSES

> *They will not go on if it be so*
> *Christmas morning though it be, it is necessary to send up*
>   *workmen*
> *They will forget before the week be out*
> *Doubt not but I will use my utmost skill, so that the Pope*
>   *attend to your complaint*

Reconciling the subjunctive's use in conditional clauses with its other uses poses the same kind of problem we have encountered in examining earlier uses of the subjunctive in object clauses. Both subjunctive and indicative occur in conditional clauses, with no apparent difference in meaning. Compare the sentences,

They will not go on if it be so.

They will not go on if it is so.

These two sentences appear to mean the same thing, but according to the analysis proposed here, they are semantically different. Semantic information for the conditional clause of the first sentence is as follows:

pres/prac (So)

Semantic information for the conditional clause of the second sentence is as follows:

pres/theor (So)

Pragmatic information is the same for each, both mood and tense reflecting the current point of view of the speaker. The reason the sentences appear to mean the same thing is simply that manner of representation is unimportant in conditional clauses. To regard a situation as a condition for some other situation is not to regard it as to be perceived, necessarily, nor as to be brought about, necessarily, but possibly as either. The purpose of conditional sentences is usually to indicate a connection between states of affairs. This purpose can be accomplished, the consequences of some state of affairs (the condition) can be pursued, regardless of the manner in which that state of affairs is represented. Since either manner of representation will do, either mood is serviceable.

Use of the subjunctive in conditional clauses is no different from use of the imperative or the subjunctive substitute with *let* and the infinitive to state the premises of an argument. If we wish to argue, for example, that a consequence of a triangle's having three equal sides will be that it has three equal angles, we can state the argument in alternative ways. We can say,

> Make the sides of a triangle equal. The angles will then be equal.

Or we can say,

> Let the sides of a triangle be equal. The angles then are
> also equal.

Or we can say,

> We suppose the following: A triangle's sides are equal. We
> conclude the following: The triangle's angles are equal.

The first alternative presents the premise in an imperative sentence, the second presents it with a subjunctive substitute, and the third presents it in a simple declarative sentence in the indicative. In the first two, the situation of a triangle's sides being equal is represented as something to be brought about, while in the third, the same situation is represented as something to be perceived. The manner of representation of the premises of an argument makes no difference in practice.

Now consider the sentences,

> If the sides of a triangle be equal, then the angles are also equal.

> If the sides of a triangle are equal, then the angles are also equal.

The first of these sentences is comparable to the pattern of argument,

"Let the sides of a triangle be equal. Then the angles are also equal."
The second is comparable to the pattern of argument, "We suppose the
following: The sides of a triangle are equal. We conclude the following: The angles are also equal." In both patterns of argument the relation between the two states of affairs is what is important, the first state
of affairs being sufficient to ensure the second. The argument can be
made no matter how the first situation is represented, as long as it is
clear that it is a supposition. *Let* with the infinitive is a current idiom
for making suppositions. The indicative in declarative sentences does
not necessarily make suppositions, but in an appropriate context (with
some preceding indication that the sentence is a supposition, for instance), it will serve the same purpose as *let* with the infinitive.
Likewise, the relation between the states of affairs indicated by the
protasis and the apodosis of a conditional sentence is what is important;
the modality of the protasis is not. The word *if* in conditional sentences
signals that the purpose of the dependent clause is to indicate a condition, and since modality does not pertain to that purpose, mood is indif-
ferent. There is no reason (except perhaps obsolescence, which for the
time being I ignore) to suppose that the subjunctive ceases to signify
practical modality in this context, or the indicative, theoretical. The
word *if* and pragmatic features of context supply the meaning 'condition', but 'condition' is not the signification of either of the moods.

Earlier uses of the subjunctive in adverb clauses are also consistent
with the view that the subjunctive signifies practical modality. Some of
the more important earlier uses are in clauses of concession, time, and
purpose. Visser cites the following examples:

> Christmas morning though it be, it is necessary to sent
> [send] up workmen. (p. 905)

> they will forget before the week be out. (p. 872)

> Doubt not byt [but] I will use my utmost skill, So that the
> Pope attend to your complaint. (p. 864)

Although none of these three uses survives, except marginally in
literary language, all are common before modern times. The subjunctive in these uses, as in conditional clauses, has never occurred to the
exclusion of the indicative, so again we must explain the variation. As
with other uses in which moods have alternated, we can attribute the
option in choice of mood to the complicating semantic effects of surrounding forms.

Concessional clauses are like conditional clauses in presenting a condition, albeit a different kind of condition. Ordinary conditional clauses represent a condition which is sufficient to ensure the state of affairs represented in the main clause. Concessional clauses represent a condition which is not sufficient to prevent the state of affairs represented in the main clause. In both conditional and concessional sentences, the relation between states of affairs is more important than the relation between the dependent clause and the world. Just as one can indicate that a state of affairs has consequences no matter how it is represented, one can show that a state of affairs lacks consequences no matter how it is represented. Compare the conditional and concessional clauses in the two sentences,

They will not go on if it be so.

They will not go on though it be so.

The subordinating conjunctions *if* and *though* signify different things, but otherwise the sentences are semantically identical.

Yet, in earlier English, choice of mood in concessionals shows a tendency not discernible in the choice of mood in conditionals. The tendency is to select the indicative when the state of affairs expressed is taken to be actual, and to select the subjunctive otherwise. This pattern of usage probably develops because subordinators like *though, although,* and *even though,* unlike *if,* can presuppose the state of affairs represented in the clause they introduce. They do not themselves convey any notion of uncertainty, as *if* does. No pattern of distinguishing the real from the unreal develops in conditional clauses because although the indicative sets up the right kind of relation between words and world for expressing actuality, the word *if* qualifies the relation by showing that the speaker does not take the relation to hold. (This qualifying effect is similar to the effect of rising intonation on the indicative mood in questions and may be a reason why *if* is used as a subordinator in indirect questions.) Because the subjunctive does not set up the right kind of relation for expressing actuality (so any notion of actuality must come from other sources), *if* may appear to have less of a qualifying effect on the subjunctive than on the indicative. Yet, *if* still qualifies the relation between words and world that the subjunctive sets up by showing that the speaker does not take it to hold, for the speaker does not ultimately intend for the world to match the words, as he ordinarily does when using the subjunctive in independent clauses and in other contexts which do not qualify modality in this way.

The subordinators *though, although,* and *even though* do not qualify the indicative by showing that the speaker does not take the relation it signifies to hold. Therefore, when the speaker does take this relation to hold, that is, when he takes the state of affairs represented to be actual, he has reason to use the indicative, and this accounts for the earlier tendency in choice of mood. In present-day English, clauses introduced by these subordinators, clauses which now exclude the subjunctive, will nearly always express certainty. Consider the sentence,

They will stay although it is so.

This sentence presupposes the situation 'it is so', and the indicative could fail to express certainty only if the speaker gave some sign that he was not responsible for what was said, if the sentence were in indirect discourse, for instance. In order not to express certainty, the speaker of present-day English must either exchange *although* for *even if,* as in *They will stay even if it is so,* or put another modal form into the subordinate clause, as in *They will stay although it may be so.*

In earlier English, when the subjunctive was still an option in clauses introduced by *though,* it was no doubt the preferred form when the speaker did not wish to express certainty, but this is to say neither that the subjunctive itself signifies uncertainty (or non-actuality) nor that the speaker uses the subjunctive only when he is uncertain. The word *though* with the subjunctive was compatible with certainty in earlier English, just as now the word *though* with the subjunctive substitute *may* plus infinitive is and as *even if* with the indicative is. Consider an example from Visser,

this same Cassio, though he speak of comfort, . . . yet he looks sadly. (p. 904)

In this sentence, the speaker takes the state of affairs represented in the concessional clause to be actual, as context makes clear (see *Othello,* II, i, 1-34). Visser provides another example by quoting a nineteenth-century grammar: ''A conditional circumstance assumed as a fact, requires the indicative. Faulty Syntax: 'I cannot say that I admire this construction, though it be much used' '' (p. 902). The view that the subjunctive should or did always express uncertainty in concessional clauses is based on the assumption that 'uncertainty' (or 'non-actuality') is the basic meaning of the subjunctive. With the assumption that the subjunctive signifies practical modality, concessional clauses with the subjunctive in contexts which imply certainty are not problematic, and about earlier usage we can make the weaker, more accurate claim that the subjunctive merely does not imply certainty.

The subjunctive comes to be the preferred form when the speaker does not wish to express certainty as a result of the kind of relation it sets up between words and world. Since the subjunctive represents the world as a blueprint does, not as a record does, it will not itself imply actuality although some qualifying element in the context might imply actuality. The indicative will imply actuality unless some qualifying element in the context shows that the relation it sets up is not taken to hold. The concessive conjunctions *though, although,* and *even though* do not provide such qualifying context, and so in using the indicative, the speaker will likely be interpreted as expressing certainty. Wishing to avoid being interpreted in this way, either because he knows the state of affairs is not actual, because he is uncertain, or because the question of actuality is irrelevant, the speaker would have reason to use the subjunctive. The qualifying effect of the concessive conjunctions on the subjunctive, on the other hand, is the same as the qualifying effect of *if.* The concessive conjunctions show that the speaker does not take the relation which the subjunctive sets up to hold, that he does not view the state of affairs as something actually to be brought about, but rather that he represents the state of affairs in the dependent clause only to show its relation to the state of affairs he represents in the main clause.

Turning to temporal clauses, the subjunctive in earlier English occurs frequently after conjunctions like *ere, before,* and *until,* but the indicative also occurs.[15] A reason for the variation is that sentences containing such conjunctions represent two states of affairs existing at separate times, and the separate times allow separate points of view. Of particular importance is that the time of the state of affairs represented in the dependent clause is after the time of the state of affairs represented in the main clause. Consequently, from the point of view of the earlier time, the later state of affairs does not exist, and to reflect a point of view established by the time of the main clause, someone might use the subjunctive. The subjunctive can reflect this point of view because in virtue of the relation it signifies, it is a forward-looking mood, and in the absence of qualifiers, it represents something not as existing but as to be brought about after the time of speaking. Consider the temporal clause in the sentence,

They will forget before the week be out. (p. 872)

The temporal clause can be described schematically as follows:

pres/prac (Out (week))

> pres - speaker: later than the time of speaking
> prac - speaker: time of the state of affairs represented in the
> main clause

The subjunctive is particularly common in temporal clauses with the conjunctions *ere, before,* and *until* because of the time relations involved, but no matter what the conjunction, the subjunctive's use can always be attributed to the possibility of viewing the state of affairs represented as something to be brought about.

The primary purpose of a temporal clause is not, however, to represent a state of affairs as something to be brought about, but to fix the time of another state of affairs. Modality is not relevant to this purpose, for two states of affairs can be related temporally no matter how they are represented. The indicative has always occurred in temporal clauses, even in those in which the subjunctive was once common, and we can find reasons for its use too. Consider the indicative counterpart of the example cited earlier,

> They will forget before the week is out.

The temporal clause can be described schematically as follows:

pres/theor (Out (week))

> pres - speaker: later than the time of speaking
> theor - speaker: time of the state of affairs represented in the
> subordinate clause

The temporal clause represents the state of affairs, 'the week's being out', in light of perception rather than action, but this manner serves equally well for showing the relative times. Furthermore, from a later point of view, the speaker will be able to say "They forgot," and he will be able to relate this event to another event, 'the week's being out', which from the later point of view is now a fact. Regarding it as such, the speaker appropriately uses the indicative, saying, "They forgot before the week was out." The speaker, using the indicative appropriately to represent a fact when time is past might find it appropriate to use the indicative even when time is not past.

Although when time is future the state of affairs represented in the temporal clause is not a fact (not in the strict sense at least), it can still be represented in light of perception. A feature of context, reference to future time, qualifies the indicative mood, showing that the speaker does not regard the state of affairs represented as actual. There is no inconsistency here because the indicative does not signify actuality. It implies actuality only in certain contexts, and temporal clauses with future time reference are not among these contexts. Using the indicative with future time reference, the speaker uses the same mood he would use with past time reference to show actuality, and consistency is reason enough for using the indicative. Variation between subjunctive and indicative in temporal clauses can be explained by noting that modality is irrelevant to the primary purpose of these clauses and that reasons for using either mood can be found.

Turning lastly to purpose clauses, the subjunctive in earlier English occurs frequently after the subordinating phrase *so that* and after the word *that* when it means 'so that'.[16] The states of affairs represented in clauses following these subordinators is later than the state of affairs represented in the main clause, so reasons for using the subjunctive are partly the same as reasons for using it after *ere, before,* and *until*. But although there is variation between indicative and subjunctive after *so that* and *that,* the variation is very often motivated. In fact, the variation is a formal basis on which some grammarians have distinguished purpose clauses from result clauses. While earlier usage is not perfectly consistent, the subjunctive is clearly predominant when purpose is meant, and the indicative is predominant when result is meant. Such a pattern of usage supports the hypothesis that the subjunctive signifies practical modality and the indicative theoretical. The conjunctions themselves do not distinguish between purpose and result and signify only that the dependent clause represents a state of affairs which follows as a consequence of something else. If that state of affairs is an intended consequence, the clause expresses 'purpose', and if an actual or automatic consequence, the clause expresses 'result'. Consider the sentence,

> do it so cunningly That my discovery be not aimed at.   (p. 931)
> 'Do it so cunningly that my disclosure be not guessed.'

The subordinate clause, expressing intended result, can be described as follows:

> not (pres/prac (Aimed-at (discovery)))

     pres - speaker: later than the time of speaking
     prac - speaker

Now consider the sentence,

     You have done it so cunningly that my disclosure is not guessed.

The subordinate clause, expressing actual result, can be described as follows:

     not (pres/theor (Guessed (disclosure)))

        pres - speaker: time of speaking
        theor - speaker

The different meanings, 'purpose' and 'result', reflect that with the subjunctive the state of affairs is represented by the clause as something for the world to match and with the indicative, as something which the clause matches.

    In current usage, we use subordinate clauses with the indicative to express intended result. An example is the sentence,

     Hurry, so that you are early.

The subordinate clause can be described schematically as follows:

     pres/theor (Early (you))

        pres - speaker: later than time of speaking
        theor - speaker

The speaker regards the state of affairs 'your being early' as something to be perceived, but context shows that the result to be perceived is intended. Context is also important in earlier English, and although variation between subjunctive and indicative is often motivated, it would be wrong to insist that *so that* or other comparable conjunctions always express purpose with the subjunctive and result with the indicative. We do find instances of the subjunctive in result clauses, as in the sentence,

     He that smiteth a man so that he die, shall be surely put
     to death. (p. 929)

And we find instances of the indicative in purpose clauses, as in the sentence,

> a man must endeavor to look wholesome, lest he makes so
> nauseous a figure in the side-bax. (p. 698)

In the first example, context makes clear that result is meant (see Exodus, 21, 12–14), and in the second the conjunction *lest,* signifying negative purpose, makes clear that purpose is meant. Examples such as these, and ones in which it is difficult to determine whether purpose or result is meant, occur because a consequence can be at once both intended and actual or automatic. A choice of mood becomes complicated in some cases because either mood is appropriate, yet a choice between moods must be made.

2.6 SUMMARY

Context determines how we interpret the subjunctive. The subjunctive is a modal form, and when modality is important for what is communicated, its meaning contrasts sharply with the indicative in the ways we expect if we assume that it signifies 'practical' while the indicative signifies 'theoretical'. When modality is unimportant, the contrast seems to disappear, but an explanation for this lies in how pragmatic features of meaning influence interpretation. The communicative function of modality varies in the uses we have considered. In independent clauses, modality is obviously important. The hearer must know how the speaker intends his words to relate to the world if he is to obtain accurate information from him. In the object clauses of complex sentences in which modality is indicated by the verb of the main clause, modality is less important. In Modern English most verbs which take sentential complements select only one mood, so mood in the object clause specifies modality redundantly. There are a few verbs, though, which can take either mood, and so choice of mood affects interpretation of the sentence as much as in independent clauses. Many verbs which now place selection restrictions on the mood of their noun clause complements could govern either mood in earlier English. Variation occurs because the speaker can select a mood which is the same as the modality signified by the main verb and so maintains the point of view of the subject of the verb or which differs from the modality signified by the main verb and so distinguishes the points of view of subject and speaker. In conditional sentences, modality in the protasis is unimportant. Other means than mood are available for indicating that a dependent clause is a condition. In other uses in adverbial clauses, modality is sometimes important. Regular, motivated variation occurs because one manner of representation is sometimes more appropriate than the other, depending on context, and irregular variation occurs because sometimes either manner will do. We can conclude that the present subjunctive signifies practical modality. This much semantic information it consistently contributes in all current and earlier uses. Semantic and pragmatic information from other sources combines with the semantic information it supplies to give it apparently different meanings in different contexts. Consideration of the past subjunctive will lend this conclusion further support.

3

SEMANTICS OF THE PAST SUBJUNCTIVE

The problem of the past subjunctive is somewhat different from the problem of the present subjunctive. Both the past subjunctive and the past indicative occur in conditional and object clauses in present-day English: compare subjunctive *were* with indicative *was* in *They would not go on if it were so* and *They would not go on if it was so* and likewise in *They wish that it were so* and *They wish that it was so*. But there is no contrast in meaning in either case, and the variation is only stylistic or dialectal, with educated speakers often considering the indicative in these uses to be incorrect. And since the subjunctive's meaning does not contrast with the indicative's in one use but coincide with it in the other, there is no question of ambiguity. The semantic problem is to determine how the past subjunctive acquires the meanings it has in these uses, that is, the meanings usually described as counterfactual condition and idle wish. The recent use of the indicative in these constructions has a historical explanation. As the old inflectional endings that distinguish the subjunctive and indicative are lost, the forms of the two moods fall together. The tendency to say *was* rather than *were* is due to analogy, for in no other verb in present-day English does such a distinction occur. In this chapter I argue that the meanings 'counterfactual condition' and 'idle wish' arise from the combination of the semantic information conveyed by the subjunctive mood, which is 'practical modality', and the semantic information conveyed by the past tense, which is 'past time'.

3.1 COUNTERFACTUALITY AND THE PAST SUBJUNCTIVE

Before analyzing the semantic combination of past tense and subjunctive mood, let us observe the effect this combination produces in the two uses under consideration. The effect is a single effect. The difference between the notions 'counterfactual condition' and 'idle wish' is only that a clause with a verb in the past subjunctive may express either a condition or a wish. The words 'counterfactual' and 'idle' get at the single effect, while the words 'condition' and 'wish' identify the two specific uses. Other terms that grammarians and philosophers have used are 'unreal' or 'unrealizable' wish or condition. These have the advantage of suggesting a unity in the two uses, but suffer, along with 'counterfactual' and 'idle', the disadvantage of being inaccurate. The situation represented in the subordinate clauses of the sentences *They would not go on if it were so* and *They wish it were so* is not necessarily unrealizable, unreal, or counterfactual, nor is it necessarily an idle thought or wish. The situation may be actually possible or even real, and while this point has often been made by grammarians and philosophers (who continue to use the terms), it is often overlooked.[17]

Because the past subjunctive can express counterfactuality, the traditional descriptive terms are not totally inappropriate, but a term that is descriptively more precise will nonetheless promote clarity. For the time being I will say that the past subjunctive expresses imagined possibility in both conditions and wishes.[18] Imagined possibility is often 'purely' imagined or 'merely' imagined, and hence unrealizable or counterfactual, but imagined possibility is compatible with actual possibility, and actual possibility is of course compatible with reality. Consider, for instance, the following sequence of sentences:

> If Sue were helping, they would finish on time. So there is hope that they will finish. Let's see if she is helping.

The first sentence, a conditional, represents two states of affairs (one in each clause), each as an imagined possibility. The next two sentences acknowledge the actual possibility of each state of affairs, and there is nothing unnatural or contradictory about the sequence. Consider also the sentence,

> I wish she were helping, but she probably isn't.

Again there is nothing unnatural or contradictory about this sentence, but the second clause explicitly acknowledges that the imagined possibility expressed in the complement of the word *wish* is an actual possibility, albeit an unlikely one.

Imagined possibility contrasts with actual possibility in the following way. For a state of affairs represented as an actual possibility, the question of correspondence between words and world is open: a correspondence between a representation and what is represented is conceived as actually possible. For a state of affairs represented as an imagined possibility, the question of correspondence is closed: correspondence is not conceived as actually possible. This does not mean that the state of affairs is conceived as unreal or unrealizable, but only that the question of correspondence is not at issue. Since the source of contrast between these two sorts of possibility is in the question of correspondence, whether the question is open or closed, it will often be convenient to refer to actual possibility as open possibility and imagined possibility as closed possibility. We can distinguish two kinds of closed possibility: a less restrictive kind, for which the question of correspondence is not conceived as open, and a more restrictive kind, for which the question of correspondence is conceived as not open. The more restrictive kind implies but is not implied by the less restrictive kind. The past subjunctive expresses both kinds of closed possibility, without itself distinguishing them, although context will usually distinguish them. I approach the question of the semantics of the past subjunctive as a question of how it comes to express imagined or closed possibility.

In accordance with the hypothesis that there are two basic modalities, we can distinguish yet another two kinds of closed possibility: closed practical possibility and closed theoretical possibility. The distinction means no more than that a state of affairs represented as something to be brought about may be something imagined (closed practical possibility) and that a state of affairs represented as something to be perceived may be something imagined (closed theoretical possibility). In view of the different intentions behind representation in the two separate manners, we can also distinguish two separate questions of correspondence. The question of correspondence for the theoretical modality, which represents states of affairs in light of perception, is "Do the words match the world?" For a state of affairs represented as a closed theoretical possibility, the question "Do the words match the world?" is not at issue: it is not conceived as open or is conceived as not open. The question of correspondence for the practical modality, which represents states of affairs in light of action, is "Will the world be brought to match the words?" For a state of affairs represented as a closed practical possibility, the question "Will the world be brought to match the words?" is not at issue: it is not conceived as open or is conceived as not open. The past subjunctive expresses imagined or closed possibility because it expresses imagined or closed practical possibility, and it does the latter as a result of the combination of its two components, past tense and subjunctive mood. Past tense qualifies the subjunctive mood to give it the effect it has in its two surviving uses.

3.2 PAST TENSE AND SUBJUNCTIVE MOOD

How then does the past subjunctive come to express imagined or closed possibility? Taking the subjunctive to signify practical modality suggests an answer. Combining the semantic content of the past tense and the subjunctive mood in the simplest way yields a notion 'past and practical', and this, I suggest, is the original meaning of the past subjunctive. The concepts 'past' and 'practical' can combine in two other ways, however, if either the temporal form (the tense) or the modal form (the mood) has the other within its scope. They can combine to represent either a situation to be brought about as something past or a past situation as something to be brought about. The original past subjunctive, simply representing a situation as both past and practical, does not distinguish these two alternatives, but sometimes context leads to one interpretation or the other. Yet no matter how the two concepts combine, they imply closed possibility.

The combination always implies closed possibility because the practical modality, being inherently forward-looking like a blueprint and representing situations as to be brought into being, implies that the question of correspondence is an open question only for situations not earlier than the time of speaking. When the temporal form has the modal form within its scope, the representation is like an old blueprint. An old blueprint represents a situation as something to be brought about at an earlier time, but since an old blueprint is not necessarily still in force, the situation it represents is not necessarily conceived as an actual possibility. The situation may be non-actual, and the potential for bringing it about may be past. It may be an actual possibility, for the old blueprint may still be in force, or it may be an actuality, for the old blueprint may have been put into effect, but the old blueprint itself cannot imply actual possibility or actuality. The question of correspondence is relevant for an earlier time but not necessarily any longer and is therefore closed. This combination of time and modality produces the less restrictive kind of closed possibility. When the modal form has the temporal form within its scope, the representation is like a blueprint for an old situation. Since an old situation can no longer be brought into being, the blueprint representing it again cannot imply actual possibility. It may be an actual situation or not, but it must be one or the other, and in either case the question of bringing it into being is precluded and therefore closed. This combination of time and modality produces the more restrictive kind of closed possibility.

The semantic effects of combining past tense and subjunctive mood are comparable to the effects of combining past tense with other forms that signify practical modality. The words *able, intend,* and *obliged,* referring to qualities and states which are antecedents of action, signify the practical manner of representation. We can better understand the effects of the combination of practical modality and past time by observing the same combination in the complements of these more specific practical modals. Consider the sentences,

Sue was able to help.

Sue intended to help.

Sue was obliged to help.

The first represents an event, 'Sue's helping', as a past ability, that is, as a past (practical) possibility. The second represents the same event as a past intention, and the third represents it as a past obligation. These sentences represent situations as old blueprints do. In them we see a combination of past time and practical modality, and the effect of the combination is to render the question of correspondence between words and world closed. Compare these sentences with their present tense counterparts:

Sue is able to help.

Sue intends to help.

Sue is obliged to help.

The present tense leaves the question open, but the past tense relegates the question of correspondence to an earlier time. Someone can utter the past tense sentences knowing that the situation represented in the infinitive complement is not actually possible or is counterfactual or unrealizable.

Such examples will elucidate the past subjunctive, unless two further considerations cause confusion. The first is that one might observe that the infinitive complements of the present tense examples do not always imply open possibility because other unmentioned circumstances might affect the question of correspondence. Sue might be able to help but intend not to. She might intend to help, but someone else might know that she will be prevented by circumstances she does not foresee. Statements like "Sue is able (intends, has an obligation) to help, but there is no possibility that she will" are not contradictory. Yet the complements of the present tense sentences will imply open possibility unless further contextual information denies such possibility. In saying that Sue is able to help, for instance, the speaker regards Sue's helping as an open possibility with respect to her ability, though not necessarily with respect to her intention. In saying that Sue intends to help, the speaker regards Sue's helping as an open possibility from her point of view, though not necessarily from his. The realizable wish or realizable condition expressed by the present subjunctive is also open possibility. A difference between the present subjunctive and the more specific modal concepts 'ability', 'intention', and 'obligation', however, is that since the subjunctive does not refer to any specific antecedent of action, the speaker using it does not regard the situation he represents as an open possibility only with respect to a specific antecedent of action, but as an open possibility generally.

A second consideration is that one might observe that the past tense examples do not always imply closed possibility because a past ability, intention, or obligation to do something does not preclude a present ability, intention, or obligation to do the same thing. Yet our past tense examples will not themselves imply open possibility, even if they are compatible with it. Because they will not, we often infer that situations represented as closed possibilities are impossible or not actual, although we need not infer this. If someone says, "Sue was able to help," we might infer in some contexts that Sue did not help or that she is no longer able to help, but the speaker could prevent such inference by following up, saying "Perhaps she still can" or "Perhaps she did." Just as the past tense examples involving ability, intention, and obligation are compatible with the present tense examples, which express open possibility, sentences with the past subjunctive, as we have seen, are compatible with sentences expressing open possibility. But the past subjunctive's compatibility with open possibility should not lead us to conclude that the past subjunctive itself implies open possibility.

The question of correspondence between words and world is a closed question for the infinitive complements of the specific practical modals in past tense contexts not because the situations represented in these complements belong to past time but because the qualities or states that the modals refer to belong to past time. The situations themselves may belong to past, present, or future time, as long as they do not belong to a time earlier than the time of the quality or state which involves their representation. Thus, if we have a practical modal in a past tense context and a state of affairs represented in an infinitive complement, the state of affairs may belong to the past, present, or future. The sentence *Sue was obliged to help,* for example, may have any of the temporal adverbs *yesterday, now,* or *tomorrow* added at the end of it modifying *help.* The temporal import of the simple infinitive is 'contemporaneous', but since practical modals are forward-looking, we regard the state of affairs as something to be brought about as of the time of the state or quality referred to by the modal. With practical modals, therefore, the temporal import of the present infinitive is 'contemporaneous or later'. With the word *obliged,* the blueprint for the situation, a situation whose time is contemporaneous with or later than the obligation, is not necessarily in force any longer. Since the obligation belongs to a time earlier than the time of speaking, the situation, which is contemporaneous or later than the obligation, may also be past, though it need not be. The word *obliged* places a backward-looking but no forward-looking time limit on the state of affairs, the limit being the time of the obligation.

The backward-looking time limit on the state of affairs represented in the complements of the specific practical modals *able, intend,* and *obliged* restricts the two possible combinations of the concepts 'past time' and 'practical modality' to the one we have been considering. Sentences with these modals with simple infinitive complements in past tense contexts are acceptable, but corresponding sentences with perfect infinitive complements in present tense contexts are not. The following sentences, in which the temporal form, the perfect infinitive, is within the scope of the modal form, are all semantically anomalous:

*Sue is able to have helped.

*Sue intends to have helped.

*Sue is obliged to have helped.

The reason for the anomaly of course is that past situations cannot be brought about in the present. These qualities and states, 'ability', 'intention', and 'obligation', which are antecedents of action, require the enactability of the states of affairs involved in their representation.

The anomalous sentences are like blueprints of past situations, and such blueprints are defective because the question of correspondence between representation and world is precluded and automatically closed. One can design blueprints which alter the world of the past, but these blueprints cannot be 'in force' in the same sense as blueprints for future situations can because there is no potential actually to rebuild the past. Yet, one can rebuild the past in one's imagination, and one can have a desire or wish to have done or been something. Desire is an antecedent of action, but unlike other antecedents of action it does not require enactability. In contrast to the anomalous sentences above, consider the sentence,

Sue wishes she had helped.

The temporal relationship between the antecedent of action, wish, and the state of affairs represented is the same as in the anomalous sentences, but this combination of modal and temporal forms does not produce anomaly. The desire expressed in this sentence cannot actually lead to action, however. We call such desires or wishes impossible or idle because there can be no question of fulfilling them. When the desire is of the sort that can lead to action, there is a backward-looking time limit on the state of affairs involved in its representation, just as there is with ability, intention, and obligation. Desire to have done or been something is idle wish because there can be no question of putting blueprints of past situations into effect.

3.3 COMBINATIONS OF PAST TIME AND PRACTICAL MODALITY

As we did before, we can describe combinations of modal and temporal concepts schematically. By observing differences in scope and in point of view, we can explain why some sentences are acceptable and some are not, and we can explain the constraints that forms signifying past time place on the interpretation of clauses containing practical modals. Sentences with the practical modals *obliged* and *wish* and the theoretical modal *known* will illustrate.

3.3.1 *OBLIGED*

Relevant lexical information for the word *obliged* is stated below:

obliged: requires a HUMAN SUBJECT and an INFINITIVE

COMPLEMENT and signifies that the infinitive complement represents a state of affairs in the PRACTICAL modality and that the state of affairs is something FOR THE SUBJECT TO BRING ABOUT

We describe the combined semantic and pragmatic information for *obliged* and its complement in the sentence *Sue was obliged to help* as follows:

past/theor (Obliged-prac (Help (Sue, someone)) (Sue))

> past - speaker
> theor - speaker
> prac - one who is obliged (Sue): for Sue to bring about

The tense of the finite verb reflects the current point of view of the speaker. It has the modal form *obliged* within its scope. The word *obliged* incorporates the point of view of the person who has the obligation, the subject of the main clause in this case. The state of affairs, 'Sue's helping', is seen as something for her to bring about. Although tense is past, the practical modal *obliged* is forward-looking, and so there is no future time limit on the state of affairs, which from the speaker's current point of view may be past, present, or future. Because the obligation is past, it is not necessarily in force any longer, and the speaker may regard the state of affairs as counterfactual or unrealizable.

Combined semantic and pragmatic information for *obliged* and its complement in the anomalous sentence **Sue is obliged to have helped* is as follows:

pres/theor (Obliged-prac (past (Help (Sue, someone))) (Sue))

> pres - speaker
> theor - speaker
> prac - one who is obliged (Sue): for Sue to bring about
> past - Sue and speaker

The tense of the finite verb reflects the current point of view of the speaker, it has the word *obliged* within its scope, and the word *obliged* incorporates the point of view of the subject of the main clause, so that 'Sue's having helped' is seen as something for her to bring about. Since the state of affairs is past from the subject's point of view, the same point of view from which it is seen as something to be enacted, the backward-looking time limit on the practical modal is violated, making the sentence anomalous.

The sentence *Sue was obliged to have helped,* unlike its present tense counterpart, has an interpretation which is not anomalous, although prescriptive grammarians sometimes refuse to recognize such an interpretation. They call such sentences incorrect because they read them as if they violated the backward-looking time limit for practical modals. They would read the sentence as follows:

$$\text{past}_1/\text{theor (Obliged-prac (past}_2 \text{ (Help (Sue, someone))) (Sue))}$$

> past$_1$ - speaker
> theor - speaker
> prac - one who is obliged (Sue): for Sue to bring about
> past$_2$ - Sue and speaker

They take the perfect infinitive as establishing the time of the helping as prior to the time of the obligation, and this is logically impossible. People uttering or interpreting such sentences, however, take the perfect infinitive deictically, as if it were a tense. They take the perfect infinitive as establishing the time of the helping as prior to the time of speaking, not the time of the obligation. Semantic information is the same, but contextual information for the notion of past time conveyed by the perfect infinitive is as follows:

> past$_2$ - speaker

This interpretation is logically consistent. (The phenomenon is essentially the same as the 'sequence of tenses' in indirect discourse.) Some prescriptive grammarians would claim that the past tense in the main clause is sufficient to establish that the time of the helping is past, but this is not so. The time of the helping is not necessarily prior to the time of speaking because the modality is forward-looking, and there is no forward-looking time limit imposed by the simple infinitive. In the sentence with the simple infinitive, the time of the helping can be earlier than the time of speaking, but no formal element in the sentence shows that it must be. Speakers use sentences with the perfect infinitive after practical modals in an attempt to establish the time of speaking as a forward-looking time limit.

3.3.2 *WISH*

Relevant lexical information for the word *wish* is stated below:

> wish: requires a HUMAN SUBJECT and an INFINITIVE COM-
> PLEMENT or a NOUN CLAUSE COMPLEMENT and signifies
> that the complement represents a state of affairs in the PRACTI-
> CAL modality

We describe the combined semantic and pragmatic information for
wished and its complement in the sentence *Sue wished to help* as
follows:

> past/theor (Wish-prac (Help (Sue, someone)) (Sue))

>> past - speaker
>> theor - speaker
>> prac - one who wishes (Sue)

The description is comparable to that for the corresponding sentence
with *obliged,* except that the word *wish* does not refer the bringing
about of the state of affairs to the subject. Since the temporal import of
the simple infinitive with practical modals is contemporaneous or later,
the combination does not violate the backward-looking time limit on
practical modals, and we interpret the sentence as expressing realizable
wish, which can lead to action. Tense shows the realizable wish to be
past, so, as before with *obliged,* the state of affairs may be past, present, or future from the speaker's current point of view.

Combined semantic and pragmatic information for *wish* and its complement in the sentence *Sue wishes she had helped* is as follows:

> pres/theor (Wish-prac (past (Help (Sue, someone))) (Sue))

>> pres - speaker
>> theor - speaker
>> prac - one who wishes (Sue)
>> past - one who wishes (Sue) and speaker

Since the state of affairs is past from the subject's point of view, we interpret the wish expressed not as something that can actually lead to action but as an idle wish, being 'enactable' only in the imagination. The

sentence is not semantically anomalous because the word *wish* does not signify that the state of affairs represented in its complement is for some particular person to bring about and so does not imply that the state of affairs is actually enactable.

3.3.3 *KNOWN*

The combination of past time and theoretical modality is quite different from the combination of past time and practical modality that we have observed in sentences with the words *obliged* and *wish*. Consider the sentence,

> Sue was known to help.

The temporal import of the simple infinitive with theoretical modals, which are backward-looking, is 'contemporaneous or earlier', and in the sentence just cited, we regard the state of affairs as something to be perceived as of the time of the knowing. Past tense qualifies the theoretical modality expressed by *known* differently than it qualifies the practical modality expressed by *obliged*. With *known,* the record of the situation, a situation whose time is contemporaneous or earlier than the knowing, is still in force. The word *known* places a forward-looking but no backward-looking time limit on the state of affairs represented in its complement, this time limit being the time of the knowing. The sentence **Sue was known to help tomorrow* (with *tomorrow* modifying *help*) is anomalous because a record of a situation cannot be 'in force' if the time of the situation is later than the time of the record. With schematic descriptions of *known* plus infinitive complements, we can compare the notion 'past and theoretical' with the notion 'past and practical'. Relevant lexical information for the word *known* is stated below:

> known: requires an INFINITIVE COMPLEMENT and signifies that the infinitive complement represents a state of affairs in the THEORETICAL modality

We describe the combined semantic and pragmatic information for the sentence *Sue was known to help* as follows:

> past/theor$_1$ (Known-theor$_2$ (Help (Sue, someone)) (Sue))

    past - speaker
    theor₁ - speaker
    theor₂ - one who knows (unspecified)

As before in the corresponding sentence with *obliged,* the tense of the finite verb reflects the current point of view of the speaker and has the modal form *known* within its scope. The word *known* incorporates the point of view of the person who has the knowledge, someone not identified in the sentence. The state of affairs, 'Sue's helping', is seen as something to be perceived. Since the theoretical modality of *known* is backward-looking, there is a forward-looking time limit on the state of affairs, the limit being the time of the knowing, which is past from the speaker's point of view. There is no backward-looking time limit, however, and so the time of the helping can be any time before the time of the knowing.

Now consider the sentence,

  Sue is known to have helped.

In contrast to the corresponding sentence with *obliged,* this sentence is not anomalous. Combined semantic and pragmatic information for *known* and its complement is as follows:

  pres/theor₁ (Known-theor₂ (past (Help (Sue, someone))) (Sue))

    pres - speaker
    theor₁ - speaker
    theor₂ - one who knows (unspecified)
    past - one who knows (unspecified) and speaker

In the sentence with the simple infinitive, the helping may be contemporaneous with the knowing, but in this sentence with the perfect infinitive, the helping must be earlier than the knowing. This is the only difference between the two. The sentence *Sue was known to have helped,* in contrast to the corresponding sentence with *obliged,* has a potential ambiguity because two interpretations are logically possible. One is as follows:

  past₁/theor₁ (Known-theor₂ (past₂ (Help (Sue, someone))) (Sue))

    past₁ - speaker

theor$_1$ - speaker
theor$_2$ - one who knows (unspecified)
past$_2$ - one who knows (unspecified) and speaker

In this interpretation, the perfect infinitive locates the time of the event from the point of view of the subject of the modal verb (the one who knows). On this reading, the perfect infinitive conveys that the event preceded the knowing, just as the perfect infinitive does in the present tense counterpart *Sue is known to have helped*. Since knowing, which embodies the theoretical modality, is backward-looking, there is no logical inconsistency in this interpretation as there is for such an interpretation of the corresponding sentence with *obliged*. Past tense in the main clause distinguishes the speaker's point of view from that of the one who knows, however, and the sentence has a second interpretation, with contextual information for the perfect infinitive as follows:

past$_2$ - speaker

On this reading, the knowing and the helping may be contemporaneous. Prescriptive grammarians sometimes object to this interpretation because we get a pragmatically equivalent reading from the sentence *Sue was known to help*. The simple infinitive shows the helping to be contemporaneous with the knowing, and the past tense in the main clause shows the knowing to be past. Since the theoretical modality is backward-looking, the knowing marks the forward-looking time limit of the state of affairs, so the state of affairs cannot be present or future.

After adjusting for differences in point of view and in the scope of the temporal and modal forms, we can show that the notions 'past time' and 'theoretical modality' combine in the past indicative to produce the same effects that they produce when they combine in the infinitive complements of modals like *known,* and likewise that the notions 'past time' and 'practical modality' combine in the past subjunctive to produce the same effects that they produce when they combine in the infinitive complements of modals like *obliged* and *wish*. But clauses with the past subjunctive, unlike those with the past indicative and unlike the infinitive complements of specific practical modals, never (or very rarely) represent a state of affairs that is past; rather, they represent a state of affairs that is present or future. Consider the sentences below:

If Sue were helping now (tomorrow), they would finish.

If Sue had been helping yesterday, they would finish.

?If Sue were helping yesterday, they would finish.

Sentences like the first two are perfectly acceptable in present-day English. Sentences like the third occur in earlier English, but in present-day English they are only marginally acceptable, if at all, and the past perfect is strongly preferred or required. That the past subjunctive expresses only or mainly present or future time is a puzzling phenomenon, one of the longstanding problems that the subjunctive has posed for English grammar. Here I will propose that the phenomenon reflects a semantic change in the past tense but not the subjunctive mood. The change is probably a result of the forward-looking character of the subjunctive mood, the relatively limited use of the past subjunctive in independent clauses, and the increasing use of *have* as an auxiliary of perfect aspect capable of expressing past time.

3.4 PAST SUBJUNCTIVE AND PRESENT OR FUTURE TIME

Historical evidence suggests that the past subjunctive has evolved from a form expressing closed possibility by way of implication—'closed' because 'past'—to a form expressing closed possibility alone. The notion 'closed' is at first merely an implication, arising in the same way that it arises in the complements of specific practical modals, while the signification of the past subjunctive remains 'past and practical'. Past tense signifies that the situation is past, and subjunctive mood signifies that the situation is to be brought about. The tense qualifies the mood by closing the question of correspondence between words and world, but the mood qualifies the tense by looking forward like a blueprint. Since neither tense nor mood has the other within its scope, either interpretation is possible. That is, the past subjunctive can be interpreted as a specific practical modal plus the simple infinitive in a past tense context (e.g., *Sue was obliged to help*) or as a specific practical modal plus a noun clause with the past perfect in a present tense context (e.g., *Sue wishes she had helped*). The difference is not always relevant, and the past subjunctive can also be interpreted as a specific practical modal plus the perfect infinitive in a past tense context (e.g., *Sue was obliged to have helped*). Yet, often the difference is relevant, and often features of context will determine one reading or the other.

   Comparing the past subjunctive with the past indicative will suggest how the past subjunctive could have come to express only or mainly present or future time. The signification of the past indicative is 'past and theoretical', and neither tense nor mood has the other within its scope. For the clause *he was there*, the combination of time and modality is as follows:

   past/theor (There (he))

In the absence of further contextual information, both tense and mood reflect the current point of view of the speaker, but when further contextual information is present, we can interpret the clause as if either the temporal form or the modal form had the other within its scope. The difference is comparable to the difference between the two sentences,

   He was believed to be there.

   He is believed to have been there.

We describe semantic information for these two sentences as follows:

   past/theor$_1$ (Believed-theor$_2$ (There (he)) (he))

   pres/theor$_1$ (Believed-theor$_2$ (past (There (he))) (he))

The first sentence presents an earlier record of a situation, while the second presents a record of an earlier situation.

   We can interpret the clause *he was there* as if tense had mood within its scope when the clause occurs in past tense contexts, as in the sentence,

   They believed he was there.

Semantic and pragmatic information for this sentence is as follows:

   past$_1$/theor$_1$ (Believe-theor$_2$ (past$_2$/theor$_3$ (There (he))) (they))

      past$_1$ - speaker
      theor$_1$ - speaker
      theor$_2$ - ones who believe (they)
      past$_2$ - speaker: redundant with past$_1$

theor$_3$ - ones who believe (they): redundant with theor$_2$

Although this sentence has a reading on which the tense of the subordinate clause (past$_2$) reflects the point of view of the ones who believe, the past perfect (*They believed he had been there*) is preferred when this interpretation is intended. Different interpretations are possible because the tense itself does not incorporate a point of view, so point of view must be determined by context. On the reading described, the past tense of the subordinate clause (past$_2$) redundantly reflects the point of view of the speaker. It conveys the same information that the past tense of the main clause (past$_1$) conveys, and the past tense of the main clause has *believe* within its scope. On this reading, the indicative mood of the subordinate clause (theor$_3$) redundantly reflects the modality signified by *believe* (theor$_2$), and since the past tense of the main clause has *believe* within its scope, we interpret the subordinate clause as if tense had mood within its scope. We interpret the sentence as meaning the same as *They believed him to be there*.

We can interpret the clause *he was there* as if mood had tense within its scope when the clause occurs in present tense contexts, as in the sentence,

They believe he was there.

Semantic and pragmatic information for this sentence is as follows:

pres/theor$_1$ (Believe-theor$_2$ (past/theor$_3$ (there (he))) (they))

    pres - speaker
    theor$_1$ - speaker
    theor$_2$ - ones who believe (they)
    past - ones who believe (they) and speaker
    theor$_3$ - ones who believe (they): redundant with theor$_2$

The past tense of the subordinate clause reflects the point of view of both the ones who believe and the speaker. Since the believing is present and the time of speaking is present, the two points of view are the same, and from the identical points of view, the time of the state of affairs, 'his being there', is past. The indicative mood of the subordinate clause (theor$_3$) redundantly reflects the modality signified by *believe* (theor$_2$), and since *believe* has the past tense of the subordinate clause within its scope, we interpret the subordinate clause as if mood had tense within its scope. We interpret the sentence as meaning the same as *They believe him to have been there.*

We would expect the signification of the past subjunctive to be 'past and practical', parallel to the signification of the past indicative. For the clause *he were there,* with neither tense nor mood having the other within its scope, the combination of time and modality would be as follows:

past/prac (There (he))

In the absence of further contextual information, we would expect both tense and mood to reflect the current point of view of the speaker, but in the presence of further contextual information, we would expect to be able to interpret the clause as if either the temporal form or the modal form had the other within its scope. The difference would be comparable to the difference between the sentences *He wished to be there* and *He wishes he had been there.* The first of these sentences presents an earlier blueprint of a situation, and the second presents a blueprint of an earlier situation.

In earlier English, when the past subjunctive still signifies past time, the clause *he were there* can be interpreted as if tense had mood within its scope when the clause occurs in past tense contexts, as in the sentence,

He wished he were there.

In earlier English, such sentences can report a realizable wish, the wish in this case being "Let me be there."[19] Semantic and pragmatic information for the sentence is as follows:

$past_1$/theor (Wish-$prac_1$ ($past_2$/$prac_2$ (There (he))) (he))

  $past_1$ - speaker
  theor - speaker
  $prac_1$ - one who wishes (he)
  $past_2$ - speaker: redundant with $past_1$
  $prac_2$ - one who wishes (he): redundant with $prac_1$

It is perhaps still possible to interpret this sentence in this way, although *He wished to be there* is more idiomatic. It is perhaps also possible to interpret the tense of the subordinate clause ($past_2$) as reflecting the point of view of the one who wishes, but the past perfect, *He wished he had been there,* is preferred when this interpretation is intended. On the reading described, the past tense of the subordinate clause is redundant, conveying no information that is not already conveyed by the past tense of the main clause. Since the past tense of the main clause has the modal *wish* within its scope, we interpret the subordinate clause as if tense had mood within its scope. We interpret the state of affairs 'his being there' as contemporaneous with, not earlier than, the wishing.

In earlier English, the clause *he were there,* can presumably be interpreted as if mood had tense within its scope when the clause occurs in present tense contexts, as in the sentence,[20]

He wishes he were there.

Schematically, this sentence would be described as follows:

pres/theor (wish-$prac_1$ (past/$prac_2$ (There (he))) (he))

    pres - speaker
    theor - speaker
    $prac_1$ - one who wishes (he)
    past - one who wishes (he) and speaker
    $prac_2$ - one who wishes (he): redundant with $prac_1$

On this reading the state of affairs, 'his being there', is past from the point of view of both the one who wishes and the speaker. This interpretation is scarcely possible any longer. In present-day English the past perfect, as in *He wishes he had been there,* is strongly preferred when this interpretation is intended.

Comparing parallel readings for sentences with the past indicative and sentences with the past subjunctive will show the important qualifying effect of past tense on the forward-looking subjunctive. With the backward-looking indicative, past tense has no important qualifying effect: a record of a contemporaneous (or earlier) situation valid at an earlier time is valid any time thereafter, and similarly, a record of an earlier situation valid at the present would have been valid at all times at or after the time of the situation it records. Recall the two sentences with *believe, They believed he was there* and *They believe he was there*. These sentences mean different things, but the difference is only in the time of the state (believing) which involves representation in the theoretical manner. From the speaker's current point of view the time of the situation (earlier than the time of speaking) is the same in each sentence. Because the mood looks backward like a record and because

tense is past, neither tense nor mood qualifies the other in any significant way. With the forward-looking subjunctive on the other hand,
past tense does have an important qualifying effect: a blueprint of a
contemporaneous (or later) situation in force at an earlier time is not
necessarily in force at any time thereafter. Furthermore, a blueprint of
an earlier situation can only be 'in force' in the limited sense that we
can rebuild the past in the imagination. Recall the two sentences with
wish, both possible in earlier English: *He wished he were there* ('He
wished to be there') and *He wishes he were there* ('He wishes he had
been there'). These sentences mean significantly different things, aside
from the difference in the time of the wishing, because the modal form
looks forward while the temporal form refers backward. From the
speaker's current point of view, the time of the situation may be past,
present, or future in the first sentence, but only past in the second
sentence.

In earlier English, the clause *he were there* can have the two interpretations we would expect it to have, and sentences like *He wished he
were there,* corresponding to *He wished to be there,* and *He wishes he
were there,* corresponding to *He wishes he had been there,* are possible.
In the development to present-day English, however, the past tense,
when combined with the subjunctive mood, has ceased to signify
'past', but has come to signify what 'past' implied, namely 'closed'.
Ignoring rare uses which are not preferred (like *if he were there yesterday* or *He wishes he were there yesterday*), we can say that the past
subjunctive now signifies 'closed, present or future, and practical'.

Uses of the past subjunctive in which mood is interpreted as being
within the scope of tense are probably largely responsible for the
change. Sentences illustrating such uses, sentences like *He wished he
were there* (present-day English *He wished to be there*) or *They commanded that he were there* (present-day English *They commanded him
to be there*), are like old blueprints of states of affairs, and the state of
affairs can be past, present, or future from the speaker's current point
of view. Past tense in these uses originally signifies 'past time', but
context complicates the interpretation of the notion 'past time'. The
state of affairs is represented as past because the state or event which
involves its representation (wishing or commanding in the examples
cited) is past. Since such states or events represent states of affairs as
blueprints and since blueprints are forward-looking, the modality qualifies the tense so that the time of the state of affairs represented in the
dependent clause may be interpreted as past, present, or future from the
speaker's current point of view. Past tense continues to imply closed
possibility, however, no matter what the time of the state of affairs

from the speaker's current point of view is taken to be, for old blue-prints are not necessarily still in force. The semantic change in the past tense that these uses have caused is a relatively slight one: instead of signifying 'past time' and implying 'closed possibility' and 'past, present, or future time' (from the speaker's current point of view), past tense comes to signify 'closed possibility' and 'present or future time' (from the speaker's current point of view). With this change, which coincides with the increasing use of the periphrastic perfect, constructed with *have* plus the past participle and providing a new form capable of expressing 'past time', we can locate unambiguously the time of the state of affairs represented in a clause with the past subjunctive in relation to the time of speaking. For clauses with the past subjunctive, we can make a strict distinction between situations which are not earlier than the time of speaking and those which are, using the simple past subjunctive for the former and the past perfect subjunctive for the latter. Since the distinction is strict and obligatory in other areas of English grammar, the change is in keeping with a general pattern of distinguishing past and non-past time.

It is not inconceivable that a similar change could occur with the past indicative, for context can complicate the interpretation of the notion 'past time' which it conveys too. Indeed, the signification of the past tense when it combines with the indicative is often obscured in dependent clauses. Consider the sequence of tenses in indirect discourse, as in the sentence,

Sam was saying that Sue was helping.

The object clause in this sentence can represent a situation that is not strictly past in relation to the time of speaking (to the time of the speaking of the main clause—call it the time of reporting). The past tense is used not because Sue's helping is conceived as occurring earlier than the time of reporting, but because it is conceived as contemporaneous with Sam's saying, which is earlier than the time of reporting. While Sue's helping must therefore have also occurred earlier than the time of reporting, there is nothing to exclude its occurrence at the time of reporting as well. The saying and helping need only be partly contemporaneous, and the helping may extend into the present and beyond. Sam's saying, on the other hand, is presumably restricted to time earlier than the time of reporting. Someone hearing the sentence would have reason to infer this, for otherwise the reporting speaker would be expected to indicate that Sam's saying was not so restricted. He would be expected to use the present tense or the present perfect, or to add a phrase, "and still is saying", or give some other indication that he means to include present time.

The reason that someone hearing the sentence would be less likely to take Sam's saying than Sue's helping as going on in the present is that nothing complicates the choice of tense in the main clause. The time of one event, Sam's saying, is related to the time of another event, the time of the speaker's reporting. In the subordinate clause, though, a third event, Sue's helping, complicates the choice of tense. The reporting speaker, knowing that the helping is still going on, may wish to choose the present tense. Yet knowing also that the helping is contemporaneous with the saying and that the saying is past, he may wish to choose the past tense. Because of a complicating third event, we get inconsistent variation in tense in indirect discourse. In present-day English, both *Sam was saying that Sue is helping* and *Sam was saying that Sue was helping* can occur. The subordinate clauses in these two sentences convey different information, to be sure, with one explicitly acknowledging that helping is going on in the present, and the other not. Yet, the contrast between the clauses is not the simple contrast between present and past that would occur if each were an independent clause. With the increasing use of the past tense to maintain a sequence of tenses, a use more common now than in earlier English, we have developed a new, contextually influenced meaning for the past tense when it combines with the indicative mood. Where before it meant only 'past', now it means 'past or (partly) contemporaneous with another event which is past'.

With the new, contextually influenced meaning of the past tense, the past indicative can express present time. Consider the sentence,

She said her name was Sue.

This sentence makes an appropriate reply to the question "What is the girl's name?" and the clause *her name was Sue* would not ordinarily be interpreted as referring exclusively to past time. (To say "I didn't ask what her name was, but what it is" would be perverse.) In fact, the past tense in a question like "What was the girl's name?" might be interpreted as asking about present time and lead to the response "Her name is Sue." Such examples show how the meaning of the past indicative can be extended in special contexts for special purposes, so that its signification is obscured. It is reasonable to suppose that something similar has happened with the past subjunctive. The development has gone farther there, for the past tense has lost its original temporal signification entirely, but this is not surprising either in view of the forward-looking character of the subjunctive mood. Because the indicative is backward-looking, the state of affairs represented in a dependent clause always belongs at least partly to the past, being contemporaneous with a state or event which involves representation in the theoretical manner. The same is not true for the past subjunctive. Furthermore, the past indicative has a very important use, surely its most frequent use, in independent clauses, in which the contextual features that complicate the interpretation of tense in dependent clauses are not present. In independent clauses, the past indicative will almost always locate the state of affairs as only past (past and not also present) from the speaker's current point of view. The past subjunctive does not have an equally important use in independent clauses, for we have far less occasion to make blueprints of past situations than records of past situations. The past subjunctive's use in dependent clauses is therefore relatively important, making it easier for what was once a contextually determined meaning to become the form's signification.

No matter what the details are concerning the semantic change of the past tense, we can still maintain that the semantic contribution of the subjunctive mood is 'practical modality'. In earlier English, the past subjunctive signifies that the situation represented is one that is for the world to match and one that is past. Now, the past subjunctive signifies that the situation represented is one that is for the world to match, one that is present or future, and one for which the question of correspondence between words and world is closed. The notion 'imagined possibility', which the combination of past tense and subjunctive mood always implies, is a very useful one, since it allows representation of states of affairs while putting aside the question of actual correspondence. Thus, it allows one to talk about states of affairs that one knows not to exist, thinks are impossible, or for some other reason wants to represent without regard to the real world. As the past subjunctive is gradually restricted to expressing present or future time and as the past perfect subjunctive gradually assumes the function of expressing past time, English develops the same temporal distinction in clauses representing imagined possibilities as in other clauses. With this development, the past tense becomes ambiguous, signifying 'past' when combining with the indicative, but 'present or future and closed' when combining with the subjunctive. But a semantic change in tense does not necessarily produce a semantic change in mood, and continuing to take the information conveyed by the subjunctive as limited to practical modality, we will be able to account for all the uses of the past subjunctive.

3.5 USES OF THE PAST SUBJUNCTIVE

Analyzing the meaning of the past subjunctive in particular uses, as before with the present subjunctive, is a matter of identifying various sources of information and showing how combinations of information produce the effects observed. Once again, we will have to take account of the qualifying effects of syntactic environment, point of view, and communicative purpose. We will also have to pay close attention to the effects of tense because past tense qualifies the forward-looking subjunctive mood quite differently than present tense does. The effect of past tense is so important in current uses that these seem to have little in common with current uses of the present subjunctive, but a consideration of earlier uses will show that the past and present subjunctive are semantically similar and that elements of context other than tense continue to have the same kinds of effects on the mood that we have observed before.

3.5.1 INDEPENDENT CLAUSES

If only it were so
Should I not play my part, I were to blame
'Twere baseness to deny my love
It were time we left our wine flagons

The past subjunctive has no current uses in independent clauses, unless we admit exclamations like the following as examples:

If only it were so!

Oh, that it were so!

The status of these as independent clauses is doubtful because they show the markings of dependent clauses, being introduced by subordinating conjunctions. Grammarians have often treated such locutions as elliptical sentences, assuming that the speaker leaves the hearer to fill out the sentence with some easily inferred clause. Thus, the first example, formally the protasis of a conditional sentence, would have an inferrable apodosis such as "things would be so much better", while the second, formally a noun clause, would have an inferrable matrix clause such as "I truly wish that", the content of which is intimated by the interjection *oh*. Treating such locutions as elliptical sentences does not take us very far, however, because we cannot show exactly what elements have been omitted. We will be able to infer precise information in some cases but not in others, and we will be able to say little about the syntactic form of the omitted elements except that they comprise an independent clause which can embed the dependent clause that actually appears in the utterance. With or without granting that they are elliptical sentences, we can better understand the locutions and the nature of what they 'omit' by looking closely at their communicative purpose.

The question of communicative purpose is the traditional question of sentence type. While many grammarians have assumed that exclamations comprise a separate sentence type, this 'exclamatory' sentence type is not comparable to the other sentence types in important ways. The purpose of the other types is either to commit the speaker to a relation between words and world or to get the hearer to make such a commitment. The purpose of exclamatory sentences, however, is to express the speaker's emotion. This difference in purpose leads to other important differences.

The other sentence types are mutually exclusive, but the exclamatory sentence type is compatible with any one of the other three. Consider the sentences,

You are early!

Be early!

Are you early?!

Be early?!

These sentences are all exclamatory and also either declarative, imperative, or interrogative, respectively. The formal marking that these sentences are exclamatory is emphatic stress, which is compatible with either rising or falling intonation. Emphatic stress in these sentences signifies that the situations they represent make a special emotional impression on the speaker, exactly what kind of emotional impression being left to be inferred from context. Emphatic stress implies that part of the communicative purpose of these sentences is just to express emotion, with the rest of the communicative purpose implied as before. Since the communicative purpose of expressing emotion does not preclude the purposes of getting words to match the world, getting the world to match words, or getting someone else to do one or the other, an exclamatory sentence may also be declarative, imperative, or interrogative, and this calls into question the need for a separate type. Furthermore, given their communicative purpose, we can explain why exclamations need not be independent clauses. While statements, commands, and questions require representation of states of affairs, and hence declarative, imperative, and interrogative sentences must be independent clauses, with both subject and predicate, exclamations can express an attitude toward anything, object or state of affairs. Indeed, one can express a general frame of mind, an attitude toward nothing specific at all, by voicing sounds, sighs or moans, for instance, and it is sometimes difficult to tell whether an exclamatory sound is conventional enough to count as a linguistic symbol or not.

In view of these considerations, it seems unnecessary to treat exclamations as belonging to a separate sentence type. Rather, exclamations are utterances which are alike only in showing the special communicative purpose of expressing emotion. Some of the more conventional exclamations may well have begun as full sentences, but they need not any longer be treated as such, since omitted parts are no longer recoverable and since their communicative purpose is not to relate or get someone to relate words and world. Consider the exclamation,

What a beautiful day it is!

This exclamation may be short for something like "Let me tell you what a beautiful day I think it is!" or "Look at what a beautiful day it is!" or "I can't help remarking what a beautiful day it is!" but since the purpose of the utterance is not to express a wish, give a command, or make a statement, as is the purpose of the expanded versions, and since innumerable expanded versions can be devised, we have no reason to insist that the utterance is an object clause in a larger sentence.

Instead of calling exclamations elliptical, we can call them incomplete. Treating them as incomplete and, hence, defective, we do not expect to be able to recover omitted forms, but we can infer what kinds of forms could be added to make a complete independent clause. To make a complete independent clause from the words *What a beautiful day it is* we would have to supply a matrix clause with a word which could take a noun clause in the indicative mood as complement. Such a matrix would contain a word of saying or perceiving. As another example, consider the exclamation,

Hooray for our team!

To make a complete independent clause from this exclamation we would have to supply a verb which could collocate with the phrase *for our team* and which would be consistent with the emotion expressed by the word *hooray*. We would infer that the complete independent clause would be something like "I am applauding for our team" or "Let's cheer for our team." When he is having difficulty interpreting an exclamation, the hearer can attempt to supply forms necessary to complete an independent clause and so 'complete the thought'. By leaving the sentence defective, the speaker emphasizes his communicative purpose. The defective sentence *Hooray for our team!* for instance, actually serves the purpose of expressing emotion better than a complete independent clause would, for the interjection shows the nature of the emotion, the phrase shows the object of delight, and nothing else is important. A complete independent clause would imply the irrelevant purpose of getting words to match world or world to match words, and this would not further and might obscure the expressive purpose of the exclamation.

We can now dismiss the subjunctive examples *If only it were so!* and *Oh, that it were so!* as not being independent clauses. The subjunctive survives in such uses because it survives in conditional clauses and object clauses, both of which are dependent. Using the exclamation mark to symbolize emphatic stress and using the slash as before to mean 'and', we can describe the semantic information for the two examples as follows:

!.if (pres/closed/prac (So))

!.that (pres/closed/prac (So))

In each case, emphatic stress shows the communicative purpose of the utterance. Falling intonation shows that the utterance is complete, but the subordinating conjunctions show that the clauses are not independent. Past tense, when it combines with subjunctive mood, signifies 'present or future and closed', that is, it signifies that the state of affairs represented is not earlier than present from the speaker's current point of view and that the speaker regards the question of correspondence between the state of affairs and the representation of it as closed. The subjunctive mood, as before, signifies 'practical modality'. We need only note that the communicative purpose of the two examples is to express emotion. Although the nature of the emotion is left vague and can only be further ascertained in context, we can deduce the following information. The attitude expressed is toward a state of affairs, since the words showing the object of the attitude constitute a clause. The speaker regards the state of affairs as an imagined possibility, since the clauses use the past subjunctive. Both examples probably express wish because if we were to try to complete the first, supplying an apodosis, that apodosis would probably represent a desirable situation, and if we were to complete the second, supplying a matrix clause, that clause would probably include the word *wish*. Such uses are still productive, as is shown by examples like the following:

If the boss were here to see this!

This exclamation, depending on context, could express either a wish or a fearful or threatening attitude, but such uses are best treated as examples of the past subjunctive in dependent clauses.

Although the past subjunctive has no remaining uses in independent clauses, in earlier English it does have one important use. That is in the apodosis of conditional sentences, as in the Early Modern English example,

Should I not play my part, I were to blame. (p. 816)

In this use, as in exclamations, the past subjunctive means 'imagined possibility', a meaning which arises from the information conveyed by mood, 'practical modality', and the information conveyed by tense, 'present or future and closed'. Taking 'to blame' as equivalent to the predicate 'blameworthy', semantic and pragmatic information for the independent clause is as follows:

pres/closed/prac (Blameworthy (I))

pres - speaker
closed - speaker
prac - speaker

With no complicating features of context, both tense and mood are interpreted as reflecting the current point of view of the speaker. From this point of view, the state of affairs, 'the speaker's being blameworthy', is not earlier than the present, the representation of it is something for the world to match, and the question 'Will the world be brought to match the words?' is closed.

The past subjunctive means 'imagined possibility' also in the following example from Old English:

gif þu wære her, nære min broðor dead. (p. 816)

This sentence has a past subjunctive in each clause. Literally translated, the sentence is 'If you were here, not were my brother dead'; more naturally, this is 'If you had been here, my brother would not be dead'. The sentence, spoken by Martha to Jesus about her brother Lazarus, describes a death that took place four days earlier (see John 11, 17–21), so the past subjunctive verb *wære* in the first clause expresses past time. The verb *nære* in the second clause may also express past time, as it would not be impossible to interpret the clause as meaning 'my brother would not have been dead'. It is more natural to interpret the past subjunctive in this clause as expressing present time, however. Past tense expresses present time as a result of the adjective *dead,* which refers to a state existing since four days past into the present, and as a result of the context in which the sentence is spoken, which describes Martha as currently mourning for Lazarus. Had the clause referred to the event and not the resulting state by using the word *die,* we would interpret the verb as expressing past time. We would translate 'my brother would not have died'. Or had the clause referred to a non-permanent state, say with the adjective *sick,* we could interpret the verb as expressing past time. We could translate 'my brother would not have been sick', and we would do so if the brother were no longer sick or if the sickness were not currently relevant. In its actual context, however, in the first clause *wære* expresses both past time and closed possibility, while in the second clause it expresses mainly or only closed possibility. At this stage of the language, before the periphrastic perfect is firmly established, it would probably be inaccurate to say that the past tense of *nære* (*ne wære*) signifies 'closed and present'; rather the tense still signifies 'past', but context complicates the interpretation of past time so much that the basic meaning of the tense is obscured. Yet, no matter how we interpret the temporal form, the apodosis expresses imagined possibility, as does the apodosis of the more recent example.

The two examples cited above make what we call hypothetical statements, but such 'statements' are quite different from ordinary statements in which the speaker commits himself as intending his words to match the world. We can better understand how hypothetical statements differ from ordinary statements and why the past subjunctive is a suitable form for making them by taking note of their communicative purpose.

As in most conditionals, the speaker's purpose is to show a relation between two states of affairs, and one can posit such a relation without granting that the states of affairs are actually possible. Whether or not the speaker grants actual possibility is an important question, however. In conditional sentences, when the condition is met, the main clause performs the same speech act it would perform when standing alone. Consider the indicative counterpart of one of our examples,

If I do not play my part, I am to blame.

The condition qualifies the modality of the main clause by showing that the speaker is committed to a relation between the representation 'I am to blame' and the world only if the condition 'I do not play my part' is met. But if the condition is met, the speaker is so committed. If the speaker wants to posit a relation between the two states of affairs without granting the actual possibility of the state of affairs, 'I do not play my part', and so without granting that the clause, 'I am to blame', may commit him to taking the words as representing the world, he cannot use the indicative, at least not without further qualification.

Using the subjunctive in the apodosis allows the speaker to avoid making the kind of commitment that can be made by using the indicative. Because modality is practical, the clause *I were to blame* cannot be interpreted as showing that the speaker intends his words to match the world as the clause *I am to blame* can. Furthermore, using the past subjunctive allows the speaker to avoid committing himself to the kind of relation that using the present subjunctive would commit him to. Because tense is past and signifies 'closed', the clause *I were to blame* cannot be interpreted as showing that the speaker regards the state of affairs as something actually to be brought about and hence as something actually possible, as the clause *be I to blame* (or *let me be to blame*) can. Tense qualifies modality by showing that the question of bringing about the state of affairs represented is not at issue. What then does the speaker commit himself to in uttering the clause? He commits himself only to taking the state of affairs represented as an imagined practical possibility, a potential that perhaps was not actually fulfilled or cannot actually be fulfilled. Taking the state of affairs in this way allows him to achieve his communicative purpose of showing a consequence of another state of affairs which he does not want to represent as an open possibility.

Other earlier uses of the past subjunctive in independent clauses include sentences like the following:

'Twere baseness to deny my love. (p. 813)

It were time we left our wine flagons. (p. 813)

Grammarians often treat such sentences as implicitly conditional, with the complement expressing a condition and the main clause expressing a consequence of the condition. Converting the first example in this fashion, we would say that it is equivalent to the sentence, "If I denied (were to deny) my love, it were (would be) baseness." Converting the second example would be awkward, but we could conceivably maintain that it is equivalent to the sentence, "If we left (were to leave) our wine flagons, it were (would be) time" (i.e., it would be a good time or the right time). In any case, the past subjunctive is semantically appropriate in these independent clauses for the same reason that it is appropriate in the apodosis of conditional sentences: it allows the speaker to represent a state of affairs as an imagined possibility.

3.5.2 NOUN CLAUSES

> *He wishes it were so*
> *Suppose it were so*
> *I wished in silence that it were not his*
> *He bad that thider were brought the quen*
> *Heo cwæð þæt heo wære wydewe*
> *It were time we left our wine flagons*

In its main surviving use in noun clauses, in the object clause after the word *wish,* there are two reasons for using the past subjunctive. One is that the word itself signifies practical modality. The other is the same as the reason for using it in the apodosis of a counterfactual conditional: the speaker wants to represent a situation as an imagined, not an actual possibility, and he can do so with the past subjunctive. The word *wish* expresses desire, and although desire is an antecedent of action, it is unlike other antecedents of action, such as intention or obligation, in the important respect discussed above: one can have a desire, but not an ability, intention, or obligation, to do something without there being an actual possibility of doing it. Expressing imagined possibility, the past subjunctive provides an appropriate means for representing such desire.

With the semantic change in the past tense, the past subjunctive in this use signifies present or future time, as in the sentence,

He wishes it were so.

Semantic and pragmatic information for this sentence is as follows:

$\text{pres}_1/\text{theor (Wish-prac}_1 \text{ (pres}_2/\text{closed}/\text{prac}_2 \text{ (So)) (he))}$

    pres_1 - speaker
    theor - speaker
    prac_1 - one who wishes (he)
    pres_2 - one who wishes (he) and speaker
    closed - one who wishes (he) and speaker
    prac_2 - one who wishes (he)

The past perfect subjunctive signifies past time, as in the sentence,

    He wishes it had been so.

Semantic and pragmatic information for this sentence is as follows:

    $\text{pres}/\text{theor (Wish-prac}_1 \text{ (past}/\text{prac}_2 \text{ (So)) (he))}$

    pres - speaker
    theor - speaker
    prac_1 - one who wishes (he)
    past - one who wishes (he) and speaker
    prac_2 - one who wishes (he)

The past perfect subjunctive is pragmatically ambiguous in the sentence,

    He wished it had been so.

We describe one reading as follows:

    $\text{past}_1/\text{theor (Wish-prac}_1 \text{ (past}_2/\text{prac}_2 \text{ (So)) (he))}$

    past_1 - speaker
    theor - speaker
    prac_1 - one who wishes (he)
    past_2 - one who wishes (he) and speaker
    prac_2 - one who wishes (he)

On this reading, the sentence reports an original sentence, "I wish it had been so." The state of affairs belongs to a time earlier than the time of the wish. The other reading is the same except that the past perfect in the subordinate clause reflects the point of view of the speaker:

past$_2$ - speaker

On this reading, the sentence reports an original sentence, "I wish it were so." The past tense of the main clause distinguishes the point of view of the one who wishes from the point of view of the speaker, and so a situation that is present from the wisher's point of view may be past from the speaker's point of view. The past perfect, the new form for expressing past time, is chosen to maintain the sequence of tenses.

One other use of the past subjunctive is in noun clauses after the word *suppose,* as in the sentence,

Suppose it were so.

Semantic and pragmatic information conveyed by this sentence is as follows:

pres$_1$/imperative-prac$_1$ (Suppose (pres$_2$/closed/prac$_2$ (So)) (you))

pres$_1$ - speaker
prac$_1$ - speaker
pres$_2$ - one who supposes (addressee) and speaker
closed - one who supposes (addressee) and speaker
prac$_2$ - one who supposes (addressee) and speaker

Such sentences always present a condition, the word *suppose* functioning semantically like the word *if* in conditional sentences. That is, the pair of sentences, "Suppose it were so. What would you do?" is semantically comparable to the single sentence, "If it were so, what would you do?" and the survival of the past subjunctive in noun clauses after the word *suppose* is surely due only to the survival of the past subjunctive in conditional clauses.

In earlier English, the past subjunctive is widely used in noun clauses after the same words that take noun clause complements with the present subjunctive, namely, after verbs of requesting, commanding, wishing, hoping, fearing, believing, and saying. Although the past subjunctive expresses closed possibility in these contexts, it is not used, as in surviving uses, because a form expressing closed possibility is required. Rather, the subjunctive mood is used either to coincide with the modality signified by the word with which the noun clause collocates or to distinguish the speaker's point of view from someone else's, and the past tense is used to maintain the sequence of tenses. In these uses, the mood of the subordinate clause is interpreted as if the tense had it within its scope.

As recently as Early Modern English the verb *wish,* expressing desire possible of fulfillment, can take a present subjunctive in its complement, as in the sentence,

he wishes all we are told be true. (p. 843)

Also, the verb *wish* in the past tense can be used to report such a desire at a later time, and the past tense of the main verb can lead to a shift in the tense of the verb in its complement. Visser cites the following example from Shakespeare:

I thought upon Antonio when he told me, and wished in silence that it were not his. (pp. 842-43)

In this sentence, spoken by the character Salerio, the pronoun 'he' refers to a Frenchman telling of a shipwreck in the English Channel, and 'it' refers to Antonio's ship. Had it been uttered, the wish at the time of the Frenchman's report would presumably have been "Be it not Antonio's" (see *Merchant of Venice* II, viii, 1-32). We describe semantic and pragmatic information for *wished* and its complement in Salerio's sentence as follows:

$$\text{past}_1/\text{theor (Wish-prac}_1 \text{ (not (past}_2/\text{prac}_2 \text{ (His (it)))) (I))}$$

> past$_1$ - speaker
> theor - speaker
> prac$_1$ - one who wishes (I)
> past$_2$ - speaker: redundant with past$_1$
> prac$_2$ - one who wishes (I): redundant with prac$_1$

The past subjunctive in Salerio's sentence is redundant, being used only to maintain a sequence of tenses. He could have reported his wish saying "I wished it be not Antonio's," just as one can report a past statement saying "She said her name is Sue." Past tense in the main clause already qualifies the subordinate clause so that the hearer knows that the situation represented in it, being contemporaneous with an earlier wish, may belong to past time. A past realizable desire is like a past ability in representing a situation as a closed possibility from a current point of view (though an open possibility from an earlier point of view). In this respect, the complements in *I wished it be not his* and *Sue was able to help* are alike.

However, using the past tense in a subordinate clause in indirect discourse has the advantage of allowing the speaker to distinguish his present point of view from an earlier one. Saying "I wished it be not Antonio's," Salerio could be interpreted as meaning "I wished then and still do," just as, saying "I said it is not his," he could be interpreted as meaning "I said then and still do." That is, the present subjunctive could be interpreted as reflecting the point of view of not only the original speaker, the one who wishes, at the original time of speaking, but also the reporting speaker (in this first person example the original and reporting speakers happen to be the same). Semantic and pragmatic information for the sentence *I wished it be not his* is as follows:

$$\text{past/theor (wish-prac}_1 \text{ (not (pres/prac}_2 \text{ (His (it)))) (I))}$$

> past - speaker
> theor - speaker
> prac$_1$ - one who wishes (I)
> pres - one who wishes (I) and possibly speaker (I)
> prac$_2$ - one who wishes (I): redundant with prac$_1$

Using the past subjunctive, Salerio avoids any chance of being interpreted as expressing a current, realizable wish, as he might want to do if he no longer wishes for the situation or no longer views it as realizable. The past subjunctive in the subordinate clause reinforces the effect of the past tense in the main clause. The redundant past tense in the subordinate clause qualifies the modality of that clause in exactly the same way that the past tense in the main clause does, but with the result that the effect of combining the notions past time and practical modality is produced within the subordinate clause itself.

Like the verb *wished,* verbs of commanding, when they are in the past tense, can take noun clause complements with the past subjunctive in earlier English. Again, we interpret the past subjunctive as if the tense had the mood within its scope. An example is the sentence,

> He bad, that thider were brought the quen. (p. 829)

We describe this sentence schematically as follows:

$$\text{past}_1\text{/theor (Bid-prac}_1 \text{ (past}_2\text{/prac}_2 \text{ (Bring (someone, queen))) (he))}$$

> past$_1$ - speaker
> theor - speaker
> prac$_1$ - one who bids (he)
> past$_2$ - speaker: redundant with past$_1$
> prac$_2$ - one who bids (he): redundant with prac$_1$

The meaning of the subordinate clause is comparable to the meaning of the infinitive complement in the sentence *He was able to bring the queen thither*. In both cases, the question of correspondence is closed because the situation is represented as a past command or a past ability. In both cases, we do not know whether the queen was actually brought thither; nor do we know whether there remains an actual possibility of bringing her thither. The difference between *He bad, that thider were brought the quen* and its present-day counterpart, *He bade that the queen be brought thither,* is also minimal, the semantic and pragmatic information for *bade* and its complement being the same except that the present tense of *be* reflects the point of view of the subject, the one who bids, and not (or not necessarily) the speaker. The clause represents the state of affairs as a closed possibility, but it does so only as a result of the qualifying effect of the past tense in the main clause. In the Early Modern English example, tense qualifies mood within the clause itself.

Verbs of hoping, fearing, believing, and saying, when they are in the past tense, can also take noun clause complements with the past subjunctive in earlier English. An example is the Old English sentence,

> heo . . . cwæð þæt heo wære wydewe. (p. 853)
> 'she said that she were widow.'

(Use of the subjunctive after verbs of saying is not common after the Old English period.) We describe this sentence schematically as follows:

$$\text{past}_1/\text{theor}_1 \ (\text{cwæð-theor}_2 \ (\text{past}_2/\text{prac (Wydewe (heo))) (heo))}$$

> past_1 - speaker
> theor_1 - speaker
> theor_2 - one who says (heo)
> past_2 - speaker: redundant with past_1
> prac - speaker

Past tense in the subordinate clause maintains the sequence of tenses. Subjunctive mood distinguishes the speaker's point of view from the subject's: the subject is committed to the actuality of the state of affairs, 'her being a widow', but the speaker is not necessarily so committed and the subjunctive mood is therefore appropriate from his point of view. The past subjunctive varies irregularly with the past indicative in such constructions, for the indicative mood is also appropriate, reflecting the modality expressed by the main verb and perhaps also reflecting the point of view of the speaker.

Earlier English also allows the past subjunctive in subordinate clause complements of the word *time,* as in the sentence cited previously (Section 3.5.1),

It were time we left our wine flagons. (p. 813)

Semantic and pragmatic information for the subordinate clause of this sentence is as follows:

pres/closed/prac (Leave (we, flagons))

pres - speaker
closed - speaker
prac - speaker

The reason the subjunctive is used in the subordinate clause is apparently that this clause represents a state of affairs as desirable. Given that the independent clause in such sentences has a past subjunctive, it may be that a past subjunctive is required in the subordinate clause, but in general a past subjunctive verb is not required in the independent clause, and sentences like the following are acceptable in earlier English:[21]

It is time we left our wine flagons.

The latter example is roughly comparable to the sentence, "It would be desirable if (one would wish that) we left our wine flagons, because it is (high) time to do so," and represents the state of affairs, 'our leaving our wine flagons', as an imagined possibility. The kind of desirability expressed in such constructions with the word *time* is not necessarily idle wish, and sentences like the following, with a present subjunctive in the subordinate clause, are also acceptable in earlier English:[22]

It is time we leave our wine flagons.

In this last example, the state of affairs, 'our leaving our wine flagons', is represented as an open possibility.

Sentences with noun clauses in construction with the word *time* are of special interest because, although such sentences occur in present-day English, the dependent clause no longer allows a past subjunctive verb. Consider the perfectly acceptable sentence,

It's time we were leaving.

Although the verb in the subordinate clause is past subjunctive in earlier English, it is past indicative in present-day English, and only the first of the following two sentences is acceptable (at least in colloquial speech):

It's time he was leaving.

*It's time he were leaving.

If we are guided by morphology, taking the verb in the acceptable sentence as indicative, and further assume that the indicative mood is unambiguous, semantic and pragmatic information for the sentence (ignoring progressive aspect) is as follows:

pres/closed/theor (Leave (he))

In the absence of subjunctive mood, the source of the notion 'closed' now lies entirely in the past tense. (For further discussion of the significance of the unacceptability of past subjunctive *were* in sentences like the last example above, see Section 4.2.1.)

3.5.3 ADVERB CLAUSES

> *He would rest if he were sick*
> *He looks as if he were sick*
> *Though he were dying, he would not send for him*
> *There was nothing more to be said till Sir Thomas were present*
> *ic com þæt he wære geswutelud*

The main surviving use of the past subjunctive in adverb clauses is in the protasis of conditional sentences, as in the example,

He would rest if he were sick.

Reason for using the past subjunctive in such sentences is that it expresses imagined possibility. The past subjunctive is restricted to conditional sentences which have an apodosis representing a state of affairs as an imagined possibility, and it is used in order to represent the condition in the same way as its consequences are represented. Semantic and pragmatic information for the conditional clause in the sentence cited is as follows:

pres/closed/prac (Sick (he))

> pres - speaker
> closed - speaker
> prac - speaker

In modern uses, the past subjunctive signifies present or future time from the speaker's current point of view, and it signifies that the clause is a representation for a state of affairs to match, but that the question of correspondence is closed.

The problem for present-day English is not so much why the past subjunctive should be used in a conditional sentence whose apodosis represents a state of affairs as an imagined possibility, but why it should remain, at least in standard dialects. The past subjunctive is no longer used in the apodosis, as it has been completely supplanted by the auxiliary *would*. The reason that the past subjunctive remains in the protasis but not the apodosis is attributable, I believe, to the different communicative purposes of dependent and independent clauses. In most cases, the purpose of independent clauses is just to commit the speaker (or get the hearer to commit himself) to a relation between words and world, and so modality is usually important. Whenever the condition presented in the protasis of a declarative conditional sentence is met, the apodosis makes a statement. If the mood of the apodosis is indicative, the apodosis makes an ordinary statement committing the speaker to the relation between words and world that the indicative mood sets up. As the subjunctive loses its distinctiveness, becoming phonologically identical with the indicative for most verbs in the past tense, it is no longer sufficient to distinguish clauses which are not intended to match states of affairs from those which are so intended provided a particular condition is met. The auxiliary *would* supplants the past subjunctive in the apodosis of 'counterfactual' conditionals because it represents a state of affairs unambiguously as an imagined possibility, just as the past subjunctive does in earlier English when it is distinctive. The protasis cannot make a statement as the apodosis can, because dependent clauses do not have illocutionary potential, so the speaker does not risk committing himself to an unintended relation between words and world by using the non-distinctive subjunctive. The subjunctive can remain in the protasis because a non-distinctive modal form cannot lead to serious misinterpretation, as long as modality is marked in the apodosis.

The past subjunctive has one other important surviving use in adverb clauses: in clauses expressing hypothetical similarity, as in the sentence,

He looks as if he were sick.

The presence of the word *if* in such sentences suggests the presence of a conditional clause, and the subordinate clause can indeed always be expanded into a full conditional. For example, we can take our example as elliptical (omitted information being recoverable), equivalent to the sentence, "He looks as he would look if he were sick."[23] Use of the past subjunctive in the conditional clause of the expanded version can of course be explained in the same way as use of the past subjunctive in an ordinary conditional sentence. One might argue, however, that the elliptical construction has become such common usage that *as if* is perceived as a single subordinating conjunction and that the word *if* therefore does not introduce a conditional clause. (To add force to the argument, one might note that *as though* and *as if* are usually interchangeable, but sentences with *as though* are not readily expandable in the same way that sentences with *as if* are.) Yet, treating *as if* as a single conjunction does not require any reanalysis of the past subjunctive. Semantic and pragmatic information for the subordinate clause in our example sentence, *He looks as if he were sick,* is the same as semantic and pragmatic information for the subordinate clause in the sentence, *He would rest if he were sick,* and reasons for using the past subjunctive are the same: the speaker regards the state of affairs represented as an imagined possibility.

In earlier English, the past subjunctive has a range of uses comparable to the range of the present subjunctive. In many cases, it is used not because it expresses imagined possibility, the notion that is so important in its two surviving uses, but because the subjunctive mood is appropriate for one reason or another and because the clause containing the subjunctive is in a past tense context. Important uses of the past subjunctive, corresponding to important uses of the present subjunctive, are in clauses of concession, time, and purpose. Visser cites the following examples:

Though he were dying, he assured himself, he would not send for him. (p. 905)

there was nothing more to be said till Sir Thomas
were present. (p. 876)

ic com . . . þ[æt] he wære geswutelud. (p. 863)
'I came . . . that he were revealed.'

In these uses, as in corresponding uses of the present subjunctive, mood has varied, but as before, we can attribute the option in choice of mood to the complicating effects of surrounding forms.

Choice of mood in concessional clauses shows the same trend for the past tense as for the present: the indicative is preferred when the speaker regards the state of affairs as actual, and the subjunctive otherwise. Consider the sentence,

if you loved me as I wish, though I were an Æthiop,
you'd think none so fair. (p. 905)

Context shows that the state of affairs represented in the concessional clause, 'the speaker's being an Æthiop', is counterfactual. The notion 'imagined possibility' is important in this clause, as it is in the conditional clause *if you loved me* and in the omitted clause *you loved me* after the word *wish*. Semantic and pragmatic information for the concessional clause is as follows:

pres/closed/prac (Æthiop (I))

    pres - speaker
    closed - speaker
    prac - speaker

Yet, the past subjunctive also occurs when the state of affairs is actual, as in the sentence,

For though Christ were beleved and taught, yet the multitude
eftsones grewe to a shameless kinde of libertie. (p. 904)

Although the indicative would be appropriate, the subjunctive is used because it too is appropriate and frequently used in concessional clauses. The past tense is used because time is past in relation to the time of speaking. Semantic and pragmatic information for the concessional clause is as follows:

past/prac (Believed (Christ))

past - speaker
prac - speaker

The choice of mood matters little in this sentence because manner of representation is not ultimately important, the purpose of the concessional clause being primarily to indicate a relation between states of affairs and not to establish the actuality of the state of affairs represented in it.

In temporal clauses, the past subjunctive occurs with the same conjunctions as the present subjunctive does, particularly those which signify that the time of the subordinate clause is later than the time of the main clause. An example is the sentence,

there was nothing more to be said till Sir Thomas
were present. (p. 876)

The subjunctive is appropriate in the temporal clause because, from a point of view established by the main clause, the state of affairs, 'Sir Thomas's being present', can be viewed as something to be brought about. The past tense is appropriate because the time of the state of affairs represented in the main clause is past and the state of affairs represented in the subordinate clause is viewed in relation to that time. The state of affairs represented in the subordinate clause may also be past in relation to the time of speaking, though it need not be. Schematically, semantic and pragmatic information for the temporal clause is as follows:

past/prac (Present (Thomas))

past - speaker: from a point of view from which the state of affairs
represented in the main clause is past
prac - speaker: from the point of view of the time of the main clause

The past indicative also occurs in temporal clauses like this one, however, and reasons for its use can also be found. The irregular variation between past subjunctive and past indicative is no different from the irregular variation between present subjunctive and present indicative in temporal clauses.

Use of the past subjunctive in purpose clauses is comparable to use of the present subjunctive in purpose clauses. The subjunctive is favored when intended result is meant, and the indicative when actual or automatic result is meant, but the pattern does not become a rigid distinction between the two kinds of result. Consider the subordinate clause of the sentence,

> ic com . . . þ[æt] he wære geswutelud. (p. 863)
> 'I came . . . that he were (would be, might be) revealed.'

Context shows that intended result is meant (see John 1, 31). Semantic and pragmatic information for the subordinate clause is as follows:

past/prac (Geswutelud (he))

> past - speaker: time of speaking
> prac - speaker: from the point of view established in the main clause

The state of affairs represented in the subordinate clause, 'His [Christ's] being revealed', is later than the state of affairs represented in the main clause, 'the speaker's [John the Baptist's] coming', and it is past from the point of view of the time of speaking. Since the state of affairs represented in a result clause is later than the state of affairs represented in the main clause, the state of affairs may be viewed as something to be brought about from a point of view established by the main clause, and so the subjunctive is appropriate, as it is in the temporal clauses discussed above, whether the result is intended or not. But the indicative is also appropriate in result clauses of both kinds since intended result may be actual result and since from a point of view established by the time of speaking, the result may be known to be actual, especially in past tense contexts. Complicating features of context cause irregular variation in the choice of mood.

3.6 SUMMARY

The past subjunctive originally signifies what the combination of its two elements signifies, namely 'past and practical'. In this respect, it is semantically comparable to other practical modals in combination with forms signifying past time. Past time qualifies practical modality by rendering the question of correspondence between words and world closed. The past subjunctive is therefore suitable for expressing imagined possibility, the concept common to 'idle' wish and 'counterfactual' condition. Because the practical modality is a forward-looking modality, the combination of past tense and subjunctive mood has produced a semantic change in the past tense. The past tense has become ambiguous, retaining its older sense 'past' when combining with the indicative, but developing a new sense 'imagined' or 'closed' when combining with the subjunctive. The perfect auxiliary *have* with the past participle has assumed the function of expressing past time. Our hypothesis that the subjunctive mood signifies practical modality helps to explain the semantic change in the past tense, and we need not assume semantic change in the mood. Earlier uses of the past subjunctive correspond by and large to earlier uses of the present subjunctive, and context has an important influence on interpretation. Often the notion 'imagined possibility' conveyed by the past subjunctive is just an incidental effect of combining past tense and subjunctive mood, but in surviving uses, in conditional clauses and noun clauses after the word *wish,* the notion is essential. As long as we assume no change in English syntax, we can conclude that the subjunctive signifies practical modality, whether it combines with present or with past tense. Consideration of the historical decline of the subjunctive and the consequences of this decline for present-day English syntax will not affect this conclusion.

4

SUBJUNCTIVE SUBSTITUTES
AND PRESENT-DAY ENGLISH SYNTAX

The hypothesis that the subjunctive signifies practical modality will also help to explain why certain forms make appropriate substitutes for it as its use declines. The need for substitutes begins to arise as early as the Late Old English period, when unstressed vowels become increasingly non-distinctive. In those uses in which modality is unimportant or in which reasons for using either the subjunctive or the indicative can be found, the indicative supplants the subjunctive. In uses in which practical modality is important, however, the indicative is inappropriate, and as the subjunctive becomes an inadequate means for signifying practical modality because of its phonological non-distinctiveness, substitutes begin to be employed. No single substitute is employed in all the uses of the subjunctive because no other semantically similar form is as general in its signification, but each substitute, at least at the time when it is first employed, shares the key semantic feature 'practical modality' with the form it replaces. In this section, I first describe the process of replacement. I then reconsider the syntactic problem of the present-day English subjunctive in light of its declining use. I suggest different ways of describing the morphology of verbs which are historically subjunctive, discussing advantages and disadvantages of the different descriptions briefly and informally.

4.1 SUBJUNCTIVE SUBSTITUTES

The most frequently used substitutes for the subjunctive are the modal auxiliaries. These auxiliaries are full verbs in earlier English, despite morphological peculiarities, and since in Old and Middle English, when they occur in contexts in which a simple subjunctive would suffice, they are often themselves inflected for subjunctive mood, they appear to be used originally as reinforcements for the subjunctive rather than as substitutes. Since the reinforcing forms signify practical modality, inflecting them for subjunctive mood is superfluous, and the inflections are non-distinctive more often than not anyway. When the reinforcing forms begin to appear distinctively in the indicative mood, they have become true substitutes, since they are then the only source of the concept 'practical modality'. That they appear in the indicative mood in contexts formerly reserved for the subjunctive is the result of the general trend to interpret non-distinctive forms as indicative. The reinforcing verbs, being preterite-present or anomalous verbs, have distinctive subjunctive and indicative forms even less often than verbs belonging to other classes, and in present-day English, none of the auxiliaries has distinctive mood forms.

Which words come to substitute for the subjunctive in any particular use is determined by the appropriateness to that use of the semantic information beyond practical modality conveyed by the word. The most frequent substitutes are *may, shall,* and *will* and their past tense forms. The meanings of the modals are already general and diffuse in Old English and become more so in later periods, but in Middle English, when they first begin to be used frequently to reinforce the subjunctive, their early meanings, in which they are specific practical modals, are still predominant. Following is a brief semantic history of each of these words.

> *may:* The basic meaning in Old English is 'to have physical ability' (compare the meaning of the related noun in Modern English, *might*). From this basic meaning, it develops a range of related senses, including 'power', 'opportunity' (that is, 'absence of prohibitive condition'), and 'permission'. It also develops its theoretical sense, 'eventuality', 'contingency', 'theoretical possibility', a sense which is usually implied by 'physical ability', 'opportunity', and 'permission'.

> *shall:* The basic meaning in Old English is 'to be bound by an obligation', 'to owe, be obliged to do'. This meaning probably arises out of an earlier, even more specific meaning, 'to be bound by a legal obligation', 'to be liable for a debt' (compare the meaning of the related noun in Modern German, *Schuld* 'debt, obligation, fault, guilt'). From this basic meaning, it acquires the senses 'necessary' (in which it is synonymous with

of the present subjunctive's range of potential meanings. While *may* and *mot* are perhaps too weak to express resolve, *let* is available as a substitute for this part of the subjunctive's range. In present-day English, usage continues to change. *Let* is firmly established, but *may* seems to be becoming archaic and literary, with the introductory expression *I hope* replacing it in common speech. Although we do not have a single form that suitably substitutes for the present subjunctive in independent clauses, together the new substitutes (and of course other less conventionalized forms of expression) cover the subjunctive's earlier range. All the substitutes, current and past, represent states of affairs in light of action, as blueprints do.

4.1.2 *WOULD* FOR THE PAST SUBJUNCTIVE IN INDEPENDENT CLAUSES

While *may* and *let* come to substitute for the present subjunctive in independent clauses, *should* and *would* come to substitute for the past subjunctive in independent clauses, clauses which form the apodosis in conditional sentences or are like the apodosis of a conditional in representing a state of affairs as an imagined possibility. The first of the two to gain wide currency is *should,* as in the apodosis of the conditional in the sentence,

> I . . . resolved, if His Highness did come again, he should see me under no disadvantages. (p. 1641)

Such sentences are common in Middle and Early Modern English, but in Early Modern English *would* becomes increasingly frequent. It supplants *should* entirely in some dialects and in the second and third persons in others. Just as *may* and *mot* do, *should* and *would* originally reinforce the practical modality of the subjunctive mood. They occur in contexts in which their original meanings of obligation and intention are appropriate, and they occur in the subjunctive mood, although by Middle English times subjunctive and indicative forms are distinctive only in the second person singular. Since the auxiliaries themselves convey the notion 'practical modality', the subjunctive mood is superfluous, and the auxiliaries begin to appear in the indicative. At this stage *should* and *would* are true substitutes. Furthermore, in the course of the Early Modern English period, the morphological second person singular indicative ending is lost as the pronoun *thou* becomes obsolete, and no distinctive subjunctive and indicative forms remain.

Forms meaning 'obligation' and 'intention' are appropriate substi-

tutes for the past subjunctive in this us
als. Although the weaker modals *could*
of conditional sentences, they add an el
them less suitable as close substitutes f
ment of meaning being the notion of po
oretical). Although I have described the
terms of a notion 'imagined possibility
from the effect of adding a modal that
Consider the sentence,

If he did not help, he would be to b

Each clause represents a state of affairs
the apodosis describes consequences of
tential or theoretically possible consequer
The clauses *he could be to blame* and *he*
state of affairs, 'his being to blame', as
the clause *he would be to blame* describe
The clauses with *could* and *might* do not
as an imagined possibility; they describe
blame' as an imagined possibility. The
semantically equivalent to the clause with
to blame, but rather to the clause with a
tional modal, *he were possibly to blame.*

Clauses with *should* and *would,* for exa
or *he would be to blame,* are more closel
were to blame. In very early uses such clau
an intention as an imagined possibility,
stronger than *could* and *might,* which in
mental ability *(can)* and a physical ability
bility. They are stronger in the sense that
directly to action while ability does not. A
as an obligation or an intention is therefore
affairs represented as an ability. Furthermor
be used frequently to replace the subjunctiv
have been generalized in meaning to the ex
quire human subjects. Once they can be app
each develops an ambiguity between a pract
Shall signifies either an inherent, necessary
of a very general kind, or prospectiveness, fi
a natural disposition, an inherent tendency,

inal notions which are their source. When such us
what a modal implies is perceived as its significa
develops its theoretical sense.

In light of the semantic histories of the modal
that there are indeterminate cases, and independer
are often such cases. There is no reason to assume
junctive substitute, does not have the same range
that it is not ambiguous between a practical and a
that it is not indeterminate sometimes as *will* is. Cons

I will help you now.

This sentence usually expresses intention. *Will* h
the helping is something to be brought about, an
qualified by an introductory formula such as *I pr*
kinds of things can be said about the indep
sentence,

I would help you now if I could.

Next consider the sentence,

It will rain tomorrow.

This sentence usually expresses futurity. *Will* ha
the raining is something to be perceived, and
qualified by an introductory formula such as *I p*
kinds of things can be said about the indep
sentence,

It would rain tomorrow if a wind came up.

Finally consider the sentence,

I will be on time.

This sentence is usually indeterminate. It can ex
futurity or a little of both, and the difference seld
indeterminate is the independent clause in the se

I would be on time if I had to be.

pres$_1$/theor$_1$ (demand-prac$_1$ (pres$_2$/theor$_2$
(shall-prac$_2$ (not (dictate (organisation, thought))))) (he))

pres$_1$ - speaker
theor$_1$ - speaker
prac$_1$ - one who demands (he)
pres$_2$ - one who demands (he)
theor$_2$ - one who demands (he)
prac$_2$ - one who demands (he): redundant with prac$_1$

The theoretical modality signified by the indicative mood of *shall* (theor$_2$) and the practical modality signified by the stem itself (prac$_2$) are in conflict, with the result that the indicative mood is ignored. We can explain the conflict (and the way in which it is resolved) by observing that use of *shall* in this construction derives from the performative use of *shall* in independent clauses, and in this use *shall* originally predicates obligation of its subject. In the performative reading of the sentence *Thou shalt not dictate thought*, the practical modality signified by the stem of the verb is interpreted as reflecting not only the point of view of the subject (*thou*) but also the point of view of the speaker. The indicative mood signified by the ending is ignored because the speaker's purpose is recognized as being primarily to place an obligation on the subject, not to describe an obligation of the subject. For the sentence *He demands that the organisation shall not dictate thought*, we can say that a performative utterance has been reported in indirect speech and that the modality of the stem of *shall* (prac$_2$) reflects the original speaker's primary purpose, while the modality of the indicative ending (theor$_2$) reflects the original function of *shall* as a predicate used to describe an obligation, a function which is not required given the original speaker's primary purpose of imposing an obligation and which apparently has been completely lost in modern usage.

We have now shown that we can restrict the modern subjunctive to the present tense and, indeed, to the present tense of main verbs. The rules with which we began and a lexical description of the subjunctive which includes the necessary restrictions will generate finite main verbs. To account for the distribution of moods in the modal auxiliaries, we note that except for *may*, in a special sense occurring only in idiomatic independent clauses with inverted word order (and even here we do not have to treat *may* as an exception), all modals take the indicative. We also revise our rule describing the class of modal auxiliaries so that *might, must, should,* and *ought* are listed as stems that can be

must, have to, be compelled to), 'right or becoming' (synonymous with *ought to*), 'sure to take place, bound to happen'. It also develops its theoretical sense, 'prospective', 'predicted', 'inferred', 'future', a sense which is usually implied by 'bound to happen' and by the other meanings as well.

will: The basic meaning in Old English is 'want, intend, be determined to' (compare the related noun in Modern English, *will*). From this basic meaning, it acquires the senses 'to be disposed to, be willing to', 'to do habitually as a consequence of a natural disposition'. It also develops its theoretical sense 'prospective', 'predicted', 'inferred', 'future' (the same as the theoretical sense of *shall*), a sense which is usually implied by 'determined' and 'disposed'.

Although each of the modals has all its special senses in Old and Middle English, the basic meanings are still most frequent, and it is often these early, relatively specific meanings which make certain of them more suitable than others as substitutes for the subjunctive in particular uses. A brief consideration of substitutes for the subjunctive in some of its important earlier uses will show that the process of replacement further supports the hypothesis that the subjunctive signifies practical modality.

4.1.1 *MAY* AND *LET* FOR THE PRESENT SUBJUNCTIVE IN INDEPENDENT CLAUSES

Modality is important in independent clauses because these have illocutionary potential. In Early Modern English times, *may* with the infinitive becomes a common substitute for the present subjunctive in independent clauses expressing realizable wish. The auxiliary *may* is appropriate in this use because its early meanings, 'ability' or 'opportunity', are practical and so capable of reinforcing the subjunctive. Compare the two sentences,

God help you.

May God help you.

May, in the second sentence, as a reinforcing form adds its own signification to the meaning of the first sentence, so that the new meaning is, literally, 'God be able (have opportunity) to help you'. It is but a short step from the old meaning to the new: anyone wishing for God to have ability or opportunity to help someone would presumably want God actually to help, for there would otherwise be little reason for wishing Him to have the ability or opportunity. The additional element of meaning does not interfere with the intended message, and the practical modality of *may* reinforces the subjunctive, making clear that the state of affairs, 'God's helping', is seen in light of action. In time, *may* in this use becomes interpreted as a special device for expressing realizable wish and loses its original meaning. In its new, specialized use, it signifies 'practical modality' and little else.

May is a fairly recent substitute, supplanting an earlier substitute *mot,* which occurs in the sentence,

so mote God make your ofspring . . . remember you. (p. 1796)

Mot, now obsolete, is the present tense of *must.* In earlier English *mot/must* has two separate meanings, both practical: one is virtually equivalent to the meaning of *may,* that is 'have opportunity, be permitted', and the other is retained in present-day English, 'be obliged'. In its first sense, it is appropriate as a subjunctive substitute for the same reasons that *may* is. As this sense loses currency, *mot* ceases to function as a subjunctive substitute, giving way to *may.*

Yet another substitute, the imperative of the verb *let,* has a meaning very similar to the meanings of *may* and *mot.* When it has the sense 'do not prevent, allow' and when the addressee is not clearly identified, *let* is virtually equivalent to *mot* and *may* and is capable of expressing realizable wish. When the addressee is more specifically identified, as in sentences like *Let's go, let* is capable of expressing exhortation or determination and not just realizable wish. Like *may, let* in time loses its original meaning and comes to signify little more than practical modality.

Forms meaning 'ability', 'permission', or 'opportunity' are particularly appropriate substitutes for the present subjunctive in independent clauses because they are weak practical modals, weak in the sense that while they refer to requisites of action, they do not themselves move to action. The present subjunctive, signifying only practical modality, can be interpreted as expressing anything from faint hope to firm resolve, depending on context. Modals like *shall* and *will* would be less appropriate than *may, mot,* or *let,* for they refer to antecedents of action which do actually move to action. Representing a state of affairs as an obligation or an intention, they are appropriate for expressing firm resolve, but not faint hope. They are too strong to capture a large part

...s which are their source. When such uses become frequent,
...odal implies is perceived as its signification, and the modal
...its theoretical sense.

...t of the semantic histories of the modals, it is not surprising
...e are indeterminate cases, and independent clauses with *would*
...n such cases. There is no reason to assume that *would,* as a sub-
...substitute, does not have the same range of meaning as *will,*
...is not ambiguous between a practical and a theoretical sense, and
...is not indeterminate sometimes as *will* is. Consider the sentence,

I will help you now.

sentence usually expresses intention. *Will* has its practical sense,
helping is something to be brought about, and the sentence can be
...lified by an introductory formula such as *I promise that.* The same
...nds of things can be said about the independent clause in the
...ntence,

I would help you now if I could.

Next consider the sentence,

It will rain tomorrow.

This sentence usually expresses futurity. *Will* has its theoretical sense,
the raining is something to be perceived, and the sentence can be
qualified by an introductory formula such as *I predict that.* The same
kinds of things can be said about the independent clause in the
sentence,

It would rain tomorrow if a wind came up.

Finally consider the sentence,

I will be on time.

This sentence is usually indeterminate. It can express either intention or
futurity or a little of both, and the difference seldom matters.[24] Similarly
indeterminate is the independent clause in the sentence,

I would be on time if I had to be.

of the present subjunctive's range of potential meanings. While *may*
and *mot* are perhaps too weak to express resolve, *let* is available as a
substitute for this part of the subjunctive's range. In present-day
English, usage continues to change. *Let* is firmly established, but *may*
seems to be becoming archaic and literary, with the introductory expression *I hope* replacing it in common speech. Although we do not
have a single form that suitably substitutes for the present subjunctive
in independent clauses, together the new substitutes (and of course
other less conventionalized forms of expression) cover the subjunctive's
earlier range. All the substitutes, current and past, represent states of
affairs in light of action, as blueprints do.

4.1.2 *WOULD* FOR THE PAST SUBJUNCTIVE IN INDEPENDENT CLAUSES

While *may* and *let* come to substitute for the present subjunctive in
independent clauses, *should* and *would* come to substitute for the past
subjunctive in independent clauses, clauses which form the apodosis in
conditional sentences or are like the apodosis of a conditional in representing a state of affairs as an imagined possibility. The first of the two
to gain wide currency is *should,* as in the apodosis of the conditional in
the sentence,

I . . . resolved, if His Highness did come again, he
should see me under no disadvantages. (p. 1641)

Such sentences are common in Middle and Early Modern English, but
in Early Modern English *would* becomes increasingly frequent. It supplants *should* entirely in some dialects and in the second and third persons in others. Just as *may* and *mot* do, *should* and *would* originally reinforce the practical modality of the subjunctive mood. They occur in
contexts in which their original meanings of obligation and intention
are appropriate, and they occur in the subjunctive mood, although by
Middle English times subjunctive and indicative forms are distinctive
only in the second person singular. Since the auxiliaries themselves
convey the notion 'practical modality', the subjunctive mood is superfluous, and the auxiliaries begin to appear in the indicative. At this
stage *should* and *would* are true substitutes. Furthermore, in the course
of the Early Modern English period, the morphological second person
singular indicative ending is lost as the pronoun *thou* becomes obsolete,
and no distinctive subjunctive and indicative forms remain.

Forms meaning 'obligation' and 'intention' are appropriate substitutes for the past subjunctive in this use because they are strong modals. Although the weaker modals *could* and *might* occur in the apodosis of conditional sentences, they add an element of meaning which makes them less suitable as close substitutes for the past subjunctive, this element of meaning being the notion of possibility (either practical or theoretical). Although I have described the effect of the past subjunctive in terms of a notion 'imagined possibility', this effect is quite different from the effect of adding a modal that signifies possibility to a clause. Consider the sentence,

If he did not help, he would be to blame.

Each clause represents a state of affairs as an imagined possibility, but the apodosis describes consequences of an imagined condition, not potential or theoretically possible consequences of an imagined condition. The clauses *he could be to blame* and *he might be to blame* describe the state of affairs, 'his being to blame', as a possible consequence, while the clause *he would be to blame* describes it simply as a consequence. The clauses with *could* and *might* do not describe 'his being to blame' as an imagined possibility; they describe the possibility of 'his being to blame' as an imagined possibility. These clauses are therefore not semantically equivalent to the clause with a past subjunctive, *he were to blame*, but rather to the clause with a past subjunctive and an additional modal, *he were possibly to blame*.

Clauses with *should* and *would*, for example, *he should be to blame* or *he would be to blame*, are more closely equivalent to the clause *he were to blame*. In very early uses such clauses describe an obligation or an intention as an imagined possibility, and in these uses they are stronger than *could* and *might*, which in very early uses describe a mental ability *(can)* and a physical ability *(may)* as an imagined possibility. They are stronger in the sense that obligation and intention lead directly to action while ability does not. A state of affairs represented as an obligation or an intention is therefore more a surety than a state of affairs represented as an ability. Furthermore, by the time they begin to be used frequently to replace the subjunctive, the words *shall* and *will* have been generalized in meaning to the extent that they no longer require human subjects. Once they can be applied to non-human subjects, each develops an ambiguity between a practical and a theoretical sense. *Shall* signifies either an inherent, necessary characteristic, a compulsion of a very general kind, or prospectiveness, futurity. *Will* signifies either a natural disposition, an inherent tendency, or prospectiveness, futurity.

In their practical senses, *shall* and w̲
because a human being who is oblig
way or a non-human thing which is
tendency to behave in some way will in
way, and so the states of affairs represe.
shall and *will* are more predictable and so
resented in clauses with practical *can* an
theoretical senses *shall* and *will* are stronger
prospects are more certain than theoretical p
and *would* do not imply uncertainty as *could*
better suited to substitute for the past subj
sentences.

In present-day English, *should* and *would* ofte
their early meanings 'obligation' and 'intention' wh
subjunctive substitutes in the apodosis of conditional
it seems likely that since *should* can mean 'obligation'
hence creates a potential ambiguity in conditionals,
should be to blame being interpretable as meaning e
(would be) to blame' or 'he ought to be to blame', it
would, whose meaning 'intention' is more easily preclude
and is less misleading in doubtful cases. But since *wou*
longer means intention (nor *should* obligation when it is me
junctive substitute), the question arises whether it continues t
practical modality in the apodosis of conditionals. If it does not,
tution has caused a semantic change.

The question is a difficult one because *would* and the other
auxiliaries in English are sometimes indeterminate, which is to say
in some contexts it is not clear whether they have their root sense,
nifying practical modality, or their epistemic sense, signifying theo
etical modality. Their indeterminacy has a historical explanation. The
theoretical senses, 'theoretical possibility' for *may* and 'futurity' for
shall and *will*, are usually implied by the verbs in their early meanings.
An ability or a potential to bring about a state of affairs will generally
imply the theoretical possibility of that state of affairs. Something may
interfere, but without specific reason for believing the contrary, we assume that a potential state of affairs is also a theoretically possible one.
Similarly, an obligation or general compulsion (necessity) and an intention or natural tendency will generally imply the future actuality of that
state of affairs. Again, something may interfere, but without reason for
assuming the contrary, we assume future actuality. These assumptions
can be very important in some contexts, more important than the orig-

With these considerations in mind, I conclude that the substitution of *would* for the past subjunctive has changed the semantics of the apodosis in English conditional sentences. *Would* does not always signify practical modality, as the past subjunctive does, and when *would* signifies practical modality, it adds the further information 'intention' or the like. The change is scarcely apparent, however, because the semantic combination produced by *will* and the past tense is the same as the semantic combination of the subjunctive mood and the past tense in expressing imagined or closed possibility, and this is the notion that is crucial in hypothetical statements. The combination of *will* and the past tense could, and perhaps once did in some instances, produce the notion 'closed possibility' much as the past subjunctive once did, with *will* representing a state of affairs as an intention (practical modality) or as a prospect (theoretical modality) or as something similar (perhaps indeterminate modality) and with past tense relegating the intention or prospect, etc., to an earlier time. A past intention or prospect is not necessarily a current intention or prospect, so the question of correspondence is not necessarily open. More likely however, since *would* begins to replace the subjunctive first by reinforcing it and so is itself a past subjunctive verb, the past tense has already undergone its change and does not signify 'past' but 'closed'. *Would* in this case represents a state of affairs as an intention or prospect which is imagined, a state of affairs for which the question of correspondence is closed. Simple *would* in this case has the temporal significance 'not earlier than present', while *would have* has the temporal significance 'earlier than present'.

Although the apodosis in modern conditionals does not necessarily represent a state of affairs as a blueprint does, the new form *would* and the old past subjunctive are semantically similar in an important respect. The notion 'practical modality' is appropriate in hypothetical statements because these statements do not claim that the words actually match the world, but practical modality is not essential. Any form capable of expressing imagined or closed possibility will do, and so the conclusion that the subjunctive substitute *would* may signify theoretical modality does not lead to a further conclusion that the past subjunctive may also signify theoretical modality. The modern and the earlier forms produce a similar effect but need not therefore be semantically identical, and nothing about the historical process of replacement is inconsistent with the hypothesis that the subjunctive always signifies practical modality.

4.1.3 *MAY, SHALL*, AND *WILL* IN DEPENDENT CLAUSES

Since dependent clauses do not have illocutionary potential, modality is often unimportant, and the choice of modal forms is often complicated, with one modality being appropriate for one reason and the other for another reason. When *may, shall,* and *will* begin to function as subjunctive substitutes, the choice is further complicated because each of these words conveys information beyond basic modality and each is sometimes indeterminate. Although use of these words in dependent clauses increases as use of the subjunctive declines, indicating that they serve to some extent to replace the mood, it is not easy to determine whether they are used only because the subjunctive is not distinctive enough to convey semantic information or because the information they convey beyond modality makes them more specific or more accurate. In uses in which the subjunctive remains productive in dependent clauses, the modal auxiliaries are at most alternatives and not full substitutes for the subjunctive.

May is an alternative to the subjunctive in dependent clauses in which the notion 'possibility', either practical or theoretical, is appropriate, or at least not misleading. Particularly common is the use of *may* in adverb clauses expressing purpose. (As in independent clauses, though, usage continues to change and *may* now seems archaic and literary.) Examples are the sentences,

whisper softly that he may not heare. (p. 1782)

I made the groom ride him, that you might see him. (p. 1782)

The subordinating conjunction indicates the communicative purpose of the clause. If the intended result represented in the clause is not an actual result or if actuality is uncertain or irrelevant, there is reason for a modal form other than the indicative. *May* is appropriate because someone who does something in order to achieve a result also does something to create a potential for that result, and because *may* is a weak modal, it is particularly appropriate when the result is uncertain or nonactual. When the notion 'possibility' is not important, other substitutes occur. *Shall* and *will* are particularly appropriate for emphasizing the prospectiveness, and sometimes the inevitability, of the intended result.

May is an alternative to the subjunctive also in noun clauses after verbs expressing emotion, as in the sentences,

I fear it may lead to nothing. (p. 1785)

I wish my patience may be strong enough. (p. 1784)

After such verbs, manner of representation, from the point of view of the subject, is already indicated by the verb. The modal in the subordinate clause can be interpreted as reflecting either the subject's or the speaker's point of view, and when possibility or uncertainty is important from one of these points of view, *may* is appropriate. When prospectiveness or inevitability is important, *shall* and *will* are appropriate.

Shall and *should* are alternatives to the subjunctive in noun clauses and are true substitutes for it in British dialects in which the subjunctive is no longer productive. Examples are the sentences,

> The memorial asks that Parliament shall make it illegal
> to vivisect dogs. (p. 1622)

> He . . . requested that a bowl of Devonshire cream
> should be passed along. (p. 1656)

In these sentences the subjunctive is replaced in environments that could retain it in American English. *Shall* and *should* have a history in such constructions that dates back to Old English. An early example is the sentence,

> Moyses us bebead on þære æ þæt we sccoldon þus gerade
> mid stanum oftorfian. (p. 1655)
> 'Moses commanded us in the law that we should such with
> stones stone to death.'

The original appropriateness of *shall* is its early meaning 'obligation'. This is also its appropriateness in independent clauses of the type,

> Thou shalt not kill.

In sentences like this, *shall* is also a subjunctive substitute or else an alternative to the imperative. *Shall* does not specify any particular type of obligation, and the source of the obligation can vary. In independent clauses, the source of obligation is often interpreted to be the speaker, as in *Thou shalt not kill,* and in dependent clauses, the subject of the verb of commanding, as in the Old English sentence cited above. Modality is important in both constructions, since independent clauses have illocutionary potential and since verbs like *command* signify practical modality. An indicative verb in the complement of the verb *command* could be interpreted as reflecting the point of view of the speaker, since theoretical modality would conflict with the point of view of the subject, and so to avoid being interpreted as meaning that the state of affairs is an actual result of the command, the speaker must use some other modal form. *Shall* is used originally because it is a practical modal and because the notion 'obligation' suits the context: a command, unless the person commanding has no right to command, places an obligation on the hearer.

Will and *would* occur as alternatives or substitutes for the subjunctive in similar environments, as in the sentences,

> I desire that you will do no such thing. (p. 1695)

> She ... faltered out her command that he would sit down.
> (p. 1709)

This use is infrequent, however. Far more important is the use of *would* in noun clauses after the word *wish* when time is future, as in the sentence,

> I wish the snow would melt. (p. 1733)

This use apparently develops late (the earliest example Visser lists is from Chaucer) and begins in clauses with human subjects, with *would* apparently still signifying intention, but when *would* comes to be used with non-human subjects, as in the example cited, it comes to signify prospectiveness, which originally is only implied. Past tense signifies 'closed and present or future', not 'past', reflecting the origin of *would* as a past subjunctive verb. Because the past tense of *would* does not locate the state of affairs as earlier than the time of speaking and because *would* signifies prospectiveness, we interpret the time of the state of affairs represented in the subordinate clause, 'the snow's melting', as being later than the time of the wishing, that is, later than present.

Unlike *would* in the apodosis of conditional sentences, *would* in noun clauses after *wish,* as in *I wish the snow would melt,* or in the protasis of conditional sentences, as in *If you would help, they would finish,* is not a substitute for the past subjunctive. It is perhaps an alternative to the past subjunctive in uses in which context makes clear that the past subjunctive refers to future time. Thus, the sentence *He comes tomorrow* can be recast as an idle wish, *We wish he came tomorrow,* and *would* is then an alternative, as in *We wish he would come tomor-*

row. Would is an alternative, however, only to the extent that *will* is an alternative to the present tense when context makes clear that present tense refers to future time. In noun clauses and conditional clauses, *would* has the same range of meaning that *will* ordinarily has; it has the theoretical senses 'prospectiveness' or 'futurity' and the practical senses 'intention' or 'willingness'. Since *would* conveys such additional semantic information and is only an alternative to the past subjunctive when such information is appropriate, it is not a full-fledged substitute as it is in independent clauses.

Two factors may account for the development of *would* into a subjunctive substitute in the apodosis of conditionals but not in the protasis or in the complement of *wish,* the two main uses of the past subjunctive in dependent clauses which survive in present-day English. First, since dependent clauses do not have illocutionary potential, modality is often not as important as in independent clauses. Because ambiguity cannot cause the hearer to misinterpret the manner in which the speaker intends the sentence as a whole to relate to the world, it is more tolerable in dependent than in independent clauses. Second, since the apodosis presents a situation which is subsequent to the situation that the protasis presents (subsequent logically, and often also temporally), it is always appropriate, though of course not necessary, to regard that situation as a prospect. Conceptually, the apodosis presents a prospect that depends on the condition presented in the protasis for its realization. The notion 'prospectiveness' is not always appropriate in this way in the protasis of a conditional or in the complement of *wish*. However, the primary communicative purpose of *would* in the apodosis is to express 'imagined possibility', not 'prospectiveness', and so the latter notion is weakened in that use. In this weakened sense, it would be possible for it to serve as a subjunctive substitute in dependent clauses, coming to signify only 'imagined possibility' and not also 'prospectiveness'. In non-standard usage *would* and *would have* do appear in conditional clauses and in noun clauses after *wish* when 'prospectiveness' or the other senses of *will* are inappropriate, as in the sentence,

if I'd of known . . . , I'd have gone after supper. (p. 1732)

In such usage *would* is a substitute for the past subjunctive, and if such usage becomes standard, the past subjunctive will lose its last two remaining uses.

4.2 PRESENT-DAY ENGLISH SYNTAX RECONSIDERED

In speaking of the two remaining uses of the past subjunctive, I assume the existence of a past subjunctive in English. Throughout, I have assumed the existence of the categories traditionally used to describe the grammars of Indo-European languages as they are usually applied to English. Here I will discuss some of these assumptions in greater detail. I stress that I make no attempt to argue for an optimal syntactic description. The question of whether present-day English has a subjunctive mood or, more generally, to what extent the English verb remains inflectcd is complex and difficult, and here I intend only to discuss a small range of pertinent phenomena in terms that are concrete. I present several alternatives, and though I admit certain preferences, I do not try to demonstrate that any one alternative is superior to the others.

First, let us make some of the traditional claims about English syntax and morphology explicit by stating them as generative rules. We can begin with the following set:

Phrase Structure:

(1)   S $\rightarrow$ NP VP
(2)   VP $\rightarrow$ V_{fin} (Complement) (Modifier)

Verb Formation:

(3)   V $\rightarrow$ $\{V_{fin}, V_{nonf}\}$
(4) V_{fin} $\rightarrow$ V_{stem} Tense Mood Person Number
(5) V_{nonf} $\rightarrow$ V_{stem} Nonf

Lexical and Inflectional Categories:

(6) V_{stem} $\rightarrow$ $\{$come, help, have, be, can, . . . $\}$
(7)   Tense $\rightarrow$ $\{$pres, past$\}$
(8)   Mood $\rightarrow$ $\{$indic, subjn, imper$\}$
(9)   Person $\rightarrow$ $\{$first, second, third$\}$
(10)   Number $\rightarrow$ $\{$sing, pl$\}$
(11)   Nonf $\rightarrow$ $\{$inf, pstptc, prsptc, ger$\}$

The first five rules describe clause structure and verb structure. They state the following information. A clause is composed of a noun phrase (subject) and a verb phrase (predicate). The verb phrase is composed of a finite verb, sometimes accompanied by complements and modifiers. A verb is either finite or non-finite. A finite verb is composed of a verb stem and a set of inflections from the categories tense, mood, person, and number. A non-finite verb is composed of a verb stem and a separate kind of inflection. The remaining six rules describe lexical categories. If the lexicon containing the morphemes of English were complete, one section of it would contain verb stems. Each entry would be listed in a phonological form and would have the category feature '[verb]' attached to it. (Other lexical information would follow.) Other parts of speech would be listed in the same way. Another section of the lexicon would contain verb inflections, and each would be listed in a phonological form, with category features and other semantic information attached. Members of the category 'tense' are 'present' and 'past', of 'mood', 'indicative', 'subjunctive', and 'imperative', of 'person', 'first', 'second', and 'third', and of 'number', 'singular' and 'plural'. Non-finite inflections are 'infinitive', 'past participle', 'present participle', and 'gerund'. The rule for forming finite verbs gives the following instruction: Find an element in the lexicon which has the category feature '[verb]'; then find an element which has the category feature '[tense]', etc.

Rules like these are probably adequate for describing the morphology of verbs in Old English and perhaps other early Indo-European languages. Important changes have taken place in English grammar since Old English times, however, and such rules are no longer adequate. In using terms like 'modal auxiliary' and 'perfect infinitive', I have assumed that English now has two structurally different kinds of verbs, simple verbs, which are inflected main verbs, and periphrastic verbs, which are phrases comprised of auxiliary verbs and a main verb. This assumption (again a traditional one though not now an uncontroversial one) can be made explicit by changing the verb formation rules. The new rules may be formulated as follows:

(3) $\quad\quad\quad V \rightarrow \{V_{fin}, V_{nonf}\}$

(4a) $\quad\quad V_{fin} \rightarrow \{SV_{fin}, PV_{fin}\}$

(4b) $\quad\quad SV_{fin} \rightarrow V_{[main]}$ Tense Mood Person Number

(4c) $\quad\quad PV_{fin} \rightarrow AuxV_{fin}$ ($AuxV_{nonf}$) ($AuxV_{nonf}$) ($AuxV_{nonf}$) SV_{nonf}

(4d) $\quad\quad AuxV_{fin} \rightarrow V_{[aux]}$ Tense Mood Person Number

(5a) $\quad\quad V_{nonf} \rightarrow \{SV_{nonf}, PV_{nonf}\}$

(5b) $\quad\quad SV_{nonf} \rightarrow V_{[main]}$ Nonf

(5c) $\quad\quad PV_{nonf} \rightarrow AuxV_{nonf}$ ($AuxV_{nonf}$) ($AuxV_{nonf}$) SV_{nonf}

(5d) $\quad AuxV_{nonf} \rightarrow V_{[aux]}$ Nonf

These rules still state that a verb is either finite or non-finite, but add that either kind of verb can be either a simple verb (SV) or a periphrastic verb (PV). A simple verb is formed as before, except that certain stems are now excluded. Eligible stems are categorized as 'main verbs': they have the category feature '[verb]' and the subcategory feature '[main]'. A finite periphrastic verb is composed of an auxiliary verb—at least one and at most four—and a main verb. The first auxiliary takes the finite inflections, and all other verbs, main or auxiliary, take non-finite inflections. A non-finite periphrastic verb is composed of an auxiliary verb—at least one and at most three—and a main verb, all taking non-finite inflections.

The category rules can be changed to accommodate the new verb formation rules. The new rules are as follows:

(6a) V_{stem} → $\{V_{[main]}, V_{[aux]}\}$

(6b) $V_{[main]}$ → $\{come, help, see, have, be, \ldots \}$

(6c) $V_{[aux]}$ → $\{V_{[aux][mod]}, V_{[aux][perf]}, V_{[aux][prog]},$
$V_{[aux][pass]}, V_{[aux][fin]}\}$

(6d) $V_{[aux][mod]}$ → $\{$can, may, must, shall, will, ough-, need, dare$\}$

(6e) $V_{[aux][perf]}$ →   have

(6f) $V_{[aux][prog]}$ →   be

(6g) $V_{[aux][pass]}$ →   be

(6h) $V_{[aux][fin]}$ →   do

As before, these rules do not generate syntactic structures, but rather they describe the organization of the lexicon, this time indicating not only major categories, but subcategories within the major categories. Verbs belonging to the subcategory of auxiliaries have the feature '[aux]', and auxiliary verbs are further categorized as modal auxiliaries, '[mod]', perfect auxiliaries, '[perf]', progressive auxiliaries, '[prog]', and passive auxiliaries, '[pass]'. The 'finite' auxiliary, with its identifying feature '[fin]', is semantically empty, serving only as a stem which can take finite inflection. Lexical entries for the auxiliaries would contain further grammatical information, such as that the perfect auxiliary *have* requires that a past participle occur after it, that the progressive auxiliary *be* requires that a present participle occur after it, and that the passive auxiliary *be* requires that a past participle occur after it. The modal auxiliaries and *do* require an infinitive.

Such grammatical information, together with semantic information, would probably be sufficient to ensure that when the rules for forming periphrastic verbs operate, the auxiliaries appear in proper order. Thus, since modal auxiliaries have no non-finite forms, they must appear first. Since the perfect auxiliary together with the past participle signifies 'completed', it cannot appear after the progressive auxiliary, which together with the present participle signifies 'in process', since this would be a contradiction, but it can appear before the progressive auxiliary, for a state of affairs regarded as in process at an earlier time can from a later point of view be regarded as completed. Syntactic restrictions or semantic constraints prevent the passive auxiliary *be* from occurring before either the perfect or the progressive auxiliaries, and syntactic restrictions on *do* prevent any other auxiliary from occurring before or after it.

Rules like the ones presented above, embodying the categories traditionally used to describe Indo-European languages, are capable of describing the syntax and morphology of the verb in present-day English, even if they are historically biased. English retains sufficient remnants of the old categories of verb inflection that we can still identify members of the categories using morphological or other formal criteria. Other rules could surely describe present-day English syntax adequately and perhaps more efficiently, but rules derived from traditional grammatical analysis are particularly well suited for describing the modern language in historical perspective. I will therefore continue to assume these rules, making as few changes as possible to them as I reconsider the syntax of the subjunctive.

4.2.1 MOODS OF NON-MODAL VERBS

As we have seen (Section 1.1), a distinctive present subjunctive can still be identified on both morphological and syntactic criteria. To recapitulate, the verb *be* distinguishes the subjunctive from the indicative in all persons and numbers, and all other verbs save the modal auxiliaries distinguish a third person subjunctive from a third person indicative. Syntactically, the subjunctive does not follow a sequence of tenses, and in negatives the subjunctive need not have the auxiliary *do,* the simple verb being preceded by *not.* The subjunctive is syntactically distinguishable from the imperative in not allowing deletion of its subject or vocative intonation and from the infinitive in requiring a subject and not allowing a preceding particle *to.* Such data provide good reason for postulating a separate present subjunctive form in standard English.

We do not have equally good reason for postulating a past subjunctive, however, since the first and third person singular forms of *be* are the only forms that distinguish the subjunctive from the indicative, and these are not always used. A syntactic criterion, inversion of word order in conditional clauses, does apply, but only with *be, have,* and some modal auxiliaries. The imperative does not occur in the past tense for semantic reasons, so there is no question of distinguishing a past subjunctive from a past imperative. I do regard the data as sufficient for postulating a separate past subjunctive form in standard English, but I also think that the data are so scanty that there is good reason for pursuing an alternative analysis. The alternative I will pursue is the one that is least different from the traditional analysis. The advantage of this alternative is that it does not require us to assume a radical change in English syntax.

The simplest way to embody the assumption that English has no past subjunctive is to state as a restriction on the mood that it only occurs with present tense. No other change is necessary. As a consequence of this restriction, we treat the first and third person singular forms *were* of the verb *be* as alternants of indicative *was*. This seems plausible, since the two forms are often in free variation anyway. We simply note that some speakers, particularly educated ones, use the alternant form *were* in certain clause types (having learned this usage as an idiosyncracy of the language). We might also note in this connection that the number of environments in which the alternant form *were* occurs is shrinking, and we might interpret this as evidence that moods (and their semantic differences) are no longer recognized as such. As an example of a construction which formerly allowed variation between *was* and *were* but now requires *was* recall the sentence, *It's time he was leaving.* The corresponding sentence with *were* in the dependent clause, **It's time he were leaving,* was acceptable in earlier English (see Section 3.5.2), but it no longer is, at least not in colloquial speech. Similarly, a construction which might be expected to allow variation between *was* and *were* but which in fact requires *was* is the following:

He's behaving like he was sick.

*He's behaving like he were sick.

The subordinating conjunction *like,* a colloquial alternant of *as if* (assuming that we can regard *as if* as a single subordinating conjunction, as suggested in Section 3.5.3), surprisingly does not allow the variation we see in the sentences,

He's behaving as if he was sick.

He's behaving as if he were sick.

There does not appear to be any semantic difference between the sentences with *as if* and those with *like* that could explain the exclusion of *were* after *like*. Rather, it appears that to the modern intuition, *were* is merely an alternant of *was* which is restricted to particular environments, these including the word *if* but not the word *like*.

With such evidence that present-day English has no past subjunctive, we might attempt to ascertain the period in the history of the language in which the past subjunctive was lost, but to do this presents difficulties. Given that the number of environments which allow the distinctive form *were* has declined sharply in recent times, we might propose that the change occurred in the development from Early to Late Modern English. We would have to observe, however, that although distinctive *were* has a large distribution in Early Modern English (the distribution of environments being virtually as large as in Old English, though the frequency of occurrence in those environments is less), the number of distinctive forms is very small. The Old English past tense plural endings (illustrated in Appendix A) of the indicative, *-on,* and the subjunctive, *-en,* have fallen together as *-en* by Middle English times. In the course of the Middle English period, differences in conjugation between weak verbs and strong verbs are obliterated as one of the principal parts of strong verbs is lost and as final *-e* is lost or is analogically introduced into new environments. The result is that strong verbs no longer distinguish subjunctive and indicative forms in the first and third person singular. Since even in Old English weak verbs do not distinguish subjunctive and indicative forms in the first and third person singular, before the end of the Middle English period, the only distinctive mood forms of the past tense which remain in verbs other than *be* are second person singular forms.

Second person singular forms present difficulties of their own. In Old English, subjunctive and indicative forms of the past tense are identical in the second person singular of strong verbs. Weak verbs, on the other hand, distinguish the subjunctive ending *-e* from the indicative ending *-est* (or, with syncopation, *-st*). However, in Late Old English the ending *-est* appears in counterfactual conditionals (see Campbell, 1959: 325). Throughout Middle and Early Modern English, the ending *-est* appears in counterfactual conditionals, though not to the exclusion of historically regular forms in *-e*. The question arises, should we be guided by morphology in such cases and call forms in *-est* indicative? For Old English, in which many distinctive past subjunctive and past indicative forms still occur, it might seem preferable to speak of an analogical second person singular subjunctive form in *-est,* to say, that is, that at least some speakers have reinterpreted *-est* as simply a second person singular ending rather than as an indicative second person singular ending. For Middle and Early Modern English, however, distinctions in form might seem insufficient to maintain a system of two moods in the past tense, and it might seem preferable to regard historically indicative forms as indicative and to regard the declining frequency of historically subjunctive forms as a symptom of obsolescence.

Complicating matters even further are patterns of word order. Subject-verb inversion is ordinarily a sign of the subjunctive, and yet we have verbs which are historically indicative in the following early Modern English sentences:

> How much wouldst thou, hadst thou thy Senses, say to
> each of us. (p. 900)

> was I now to disappoint the young creature, her death would
> be the consequence. (p. 900)

These sentences illustrate that neither the historically indicative second person singular ending -*est* nor the historically indicative form *was* prevents the inversion typically associated with the subjunctive, although, by contrast, present-day English does not allow inversion of historically indicative forms (we say *Were she allowed to come, she would* but not **Was she allowed to come, she would*). The inversion we see in *hadst thou* and *was I* in the Early Modern English examples could be considered evidence either that English has analogical past subjunctive forms which are phonologically identical with indicative forms (such forms occurring as early as Late Old English) or that English lost its past subjunctive in the course of the Middle English period, with the residual form *were* being merely an alternant of indicative *was,* albeit a very widely distributed alternant.

Putting aside the unresolved question of when the loss of the past subjunctive may have taken place and focusing on present-day English, we must still decide whether we can adequately describe the semantics of all clauses which contain past tense verbs without reference to a subjunctive mood. I suggest that we can, that we can describe the historical subjunctive in its two important residual uses in conditional clauses and in noun clauses after the word *wish* as an indicative signifying theoretical modality.

In calling historically subjunctive forms indicative and saying that the indicative continues to signify theoretical modality, we are claiming a semantic change in the two uses under consideration. We could avoid this claim by analyzing the indicative as ambiguous, with one sense signifying practical modality and the other theoretical modality, but this claim would be dubious and of little interest even if it could be maintained. The claim would be of little interest because it would not be significantly different from an analysis which retained a past subjunctive. If we wish to say that historically subjunctive forms signify 'present or future, closed, and practical', we might as well continue to call them subjunctives, especially since formal criteria can still distinguish them from indicative forms. The claim would be dubious because while there is clear reason to call the tense ambiguous in contexts in which these historically subjunctive forms occur, there is no clear reason to call the mood ambiguous. Hearing the clause, *if they were there,* we are left in doubt about the signification of past tense. The next word could be either *yesterday* (indicating that the tense signifies 'earlier than present') or *now* or *tomorrow* (indicating that the tense signifies 'not earlier than present'). We do not have comparable doubts about modality. Such doubts could be caused by a noun clause following *insist,* as in *She insists that they come early,* in which we could interpret mood as signifying either 'practical' or 'theoretical', but we do not have comparable doubts about *were* in the conditional clause.

If we are going to call the indicative ambiguous, it seems far more justifiable to say that it is ambiguous between a general sense 'theoretical' and a special sense 'theoretical and closed' (or simply 'closed'). Whether we assign the notion 'closed' to the tense or the mood is a matter of indifference as far as the semantics of the clause is concerned. Yet it seems preferable to assign the notion to the tense because the original signification of the tense, namely, 'past', first implies the notion 'closed'. It seems more natural to say that an old implication of the tense becomes its new signification and so to assign the notion 'closed' to the form that originally produced it. Furthermore, if we were to assign the notion 'closed' to a mood, we could conceivably assign it to the old subjunctive, saying that it had a general sense 'practical' and a special sense 'practical and closed' (or simply 'closed'). But then in earlier English, in which the past tense, when combined with the subjunctive, could be used in a clause referring to a time either earlier or not earlier than the time of speaking, we would have to say that the notion 'closed and practical' arises from the combination of a tense, signifying 'earlier or not earlier than present time' and a mood signifying 'closed and practical'. The notion 'earlier or not earlier than present time' would be a very peculiar signification for a tense, and again it seems preferable to say that tense accounts for the notion 'closed', although at this stage of the language the notion is still only implied. To say that mood (either subjunctive or indicative) signifies 'closed' amounts to assuming that tense makes no semantic contribution to the construction, but there is no reason to assume this.

In any case, the notion 'theoretical' in idle wishes and counterfactual conditions is the main issue. If we can show that this notion is compatible with these two uses, we can reconcile them with other uses of the indicative and so justify an analysis that restricts the subjunctive to present tense. Our account of the semantics of *would* in the apodosis of conditional sentences suggests that there is no incompatibility between theoretical modality and the notion 'closed possibility'. A consideration of context and communicative purpose will show that theoretical modality need not be excluded from the complements of *wish* or the protasis of conditional sentences with *would* in the apodosis. After the word *wish*, manner of representation is redundant because the word itself signifies practical modality. Although a practical form may be more appropriate, it is not ultimately essential. Essential is that realizable wish be distinguished from 'idle' wish, and this can be done regardless of manner of representation. In modern usage, the word *wish* now usually takes an infinitive or double complement when it refers to realizable wish, as in *I wish to go* or *I wish him well,* but it usually takes a noun clause complement in which past tense signifies 'closed and present or future' when it refers to wish which is not or may not be realizable, as in *I wish he was (were) with us, but he isn't,* in which the wish is not realizable, or *I wish he was (were) here now, but he probably isn't,* in which the wish may not be realizable. In conditional clauses, manner of representation is not important, but distinguishing realizable condition from 'counterfactual' condition is. This too can be done even if manner of representation is theoretical. In modern usage, a realizable condition, one that is represented as an open possibility, accompanies an independent clause in which past tense signifies past time, as in *If he was there, she was there,* but a condition which is not or may not be realizable, one that is represented as a closed possibility, accompanies an independent clause containing a modal auxiliary in which past tense signifies 'closed and present or future', as in *If he was (were) with us now, I would be happy,* in which the condition is contrary to fact, or *If he was (were) here now, I would be surprised,* in which the condition is not necessarily realizable. In both 'idle' wishes and 'counterfactual' conditions, the essential concept 'closed' is retained, although the manner of representation may have changed from practical to theoretical.

Because people have the capacity to imagine the world as other than it is, they will attempt to find ways to express imagined wish and condition. Because people have frequent occasion to express such wishes and conditions, many if not all languages will have special ways of expressing 'imagined' or 'closed' possibility, and some of these ways will involve special grammatical forms. But these special ways will not necessarily be the same ways, nor will the special forms necessarily be

semantically identical.[25] That English once used the past subjunctive to
express this notion and that the subjunctive signifies practical modality
does not imply a necessary connection between practical modality and
imagined possibility. English has other ways of expressing the concept.
One way is simply to state at the outset that one is imagining things.
For example, one can express imagined wish in the following way:
"Imagine a world in which there is no hunger. We all wish our world
were like this." The situation, 'there is no hunger', is an imagined possibility, but is represented in the theoretical manner by the indicative
mood. Similarly, one can express imagined condition in the following
way: "Suppose this, which we know is not true: there is no hunger in
the world. We might conclude that there would be less strife." Again,
we have an imagined possibility represented in the theoretical manner.
Since a state of affairs represented as an imagined possibility may be
represented in either the practical or the theoretical modality, nothing
prevents us from assuming a semantic change in English counterfactual
conditions and idle wishes.

4.2.2 MOODS OF MODAL AUXILIARIES

If we can take the historical past subjunctive expressing idle wish
and counterfactual condition as an indicative in present-day English,
there is no obstacle to limiting the subjunctive to present tense except
perhaps the modal auxiliaries. According to the assumptions expressed
in our rules, the auxiliaries take finite verb endings. Once the subjunctive is restricted to present tense, the past tense forms *could, might,
must, should, would,* and *ought* are automatically indicative. Before attempting to determine whether this consequence prevents us from limiting the subjunctive to the present tense, let us consider the assumption
that the auxiliaries are finite verbs.

First, recall that our rules reflect traditional assumptions. We could
easily alter these assumptions and say that the modal auxiliaries are not
verbs or are not finite verbs and so are not inflected for tense, mood,
person, and number. To capture the new assumption, we would change
the verb formation rules so that periphrastic finite verbs would begin either with a modal auxiliary or with a finite auxiliary. The new rule
(assuming modals are verbs) is as follows:

(4c') $PV_{fin} \rightarrow \{V_{[aux][mod]} (AuxV_{nonf}), AuxV_{fin}\}$
$(AuxV_{nonf}) (AuxV_{nonf}) SV_{nonf}$

This new rule states that modals are uninflected. All historically past tense forms would therefore have to be listed in the lexicon. The new lexical rule would be as follows:

(6d') $V_{[aux][mod]}$ →   {can, could, may, might, must, shall, should, will, would, ought, need, dare}

Each would then be defined separately.

The revision has a great deal to recommend it. Although we must now define the historically past tense forms separately, we often have independent reason for doing so. For instance, *should* in its practical sense often is not simply a past tense form of *shall*. Consider the sentence,

> You should do it.

In this sentence, which is paraphrasable as "There are good reasons for you to do it," the historical past tense of *should* has no apparent semantic function. It does not signify that the 'doing it' is past or that the reasons for the 'doing it' are past. It does not signify that the 'doing it' or the reasons for the 'doing it' are an imagined possibility either. Since the historical tense has neither of its two significations, we have grounds for saying that it has ceased to function as a tense in the modern language. Similarly *might* in its theoretical sense often is not simply a past tense form of *may*. Consider the sentence,

> He might do it.

In this sentence, paraphrasable as "It is possible that he will do it", the historical past tense again signifies neither 'past' nor 'closed'. These senses of *should* and *might* can be explained by deriving them from uses of *should* and *might* in hypothetical statements, in which past tense does signify 'closed': when conditions attaching to a hypothetical statement are not stated explicitly, the grammatical form of the modal becomes obscure, and the technically past subjunctive *should* and *might* become reinterpreted as unanalyzable forms rather than as combinations of stems and inflections. With this account of their development, there is no need to insist that *should* and *might* still take finite inflections.

The lexical descriptions for the modals will be very complicated whether we treat the words as taking tense inflections or not. Furthermore, the modals have no phonologically distinctive forms for mood, person, or number. With the revised assumptions, the question

"What is the mood of the modal auxiliary?" does not arise, and we could conclude that it is possible to analyze the present-day English subjunctive as restricted to present tense. Yet, even though it is plausible to analyze the modern modals as not taking finite inflections (indeed, they stopped taking non-finite inflections long ago), it will be worthwhile to consider an analysis which does not alter the traditional assumptions. It is true that in some cases the historical past tense has no independent semantic function (that is, the historical past tense does not signify 'past' or 'closed' as it does elsewhere), and if we did say that *should* and *might* in the senses described above were inflected for tense, we would say on semantic grounds that tense was present. (This would require a slight revision in our rules.) Yet, in other cases the historical past tense does have an independent semantic function. For instance, *could* is often simply a past tense form of *can,* as in the sentences,

He could do it when he was younger.

He could do it if he tried.

In the first sentence, which is paraphrasable as "He was able to do it when he was younger," the historical past tense signifies past time. In the second sentence, which is paraphrasable as "He would be able to do it if he tried," the historical past tense signifies 'present or future and closed'. These examples, in which the historical past tense has its usual semantic functions, are grounds for saying that the modal auxiliaries still take finite inflections.

With these grounds for assuming that the modal auxiliaries are finite verbs, let us resume our analysis in which the subjunctive is limited to the present tense and consider the claim that is thereby entailed, namely, that the past tense forms of the modal auxiliaries are always indicative. The forms we are interested in now are forms which are truly past tense forms in the modern language, those for which the tense signifies either 'past' or 'present or future and closed'. Later we will analyze historically past tense forms which are semantically present tense, revising our rules to accommodate them, and take up questions of mood in modals which are morphologically present tense.

Forms in which the past tense signifies 'past' are no problem because in most cases these are originally indicative, and there is no reason to assume a change. The form *could* in *He could do it when he was younger* is composed of a stem 'can' and a finite inflection, 'past indicative third singular'. Semantic and pragmatic information for the main clause is as follows:

past/theor (Can-prac (Do (he, it)) (he))

        past - speaker
        theor - speaker
        prac - subject

The tense and the mood we interpret routinely as reflecting the speaker's point of view, the tense showing that the speaker regards the ability as something past and the mood showing that he intends the clause as a record, with words intended to match the world. Similarly the form *would* in *He believed it would rain* is the combination 'will' and 'past indicative third singular'. Semantic and pragmatic information for the subordinate clause is as follows:

past/theor$_1$ (Will-theor$_2$ (Rain))

        past - speaker: redundant with the past tense of *believed*
        theor$_1$ - speaker: redundant with the modality signified by *believed*
        theor$_2$ - subject

Past tense is used to maintain the sequence of tenses, but it still signifies 'past'. In earlier English the subjunctive could be used in indirect discourse, but since in the modern language the indicative occurs with all other verbs, there is no reason to assume that it does not also occur with the modal auxiliaries.

    Forms in which the past tense signifies 'closed' are a potential problem because these forms are historically past subjunctive, and to assume that they are past indicative in the modern language is to assume a change. Yet, as we noted in the last section, to call *would* (or *should*) a subjunctive substitute is already to assume some change. If we say that *would* is a subjunctive form, it cannot be said to have replaced the subjunctive since the subjunctive still occurs, and it can only be said to reinforce the subjunctive by adding its own semantic content. In fact, only when *would* begins to appear distinctively in the indicative do we have a criterion for determining that it functions as a substitute. The only distinctively indicative form of *would,* the second person singular form in -*est,* does occur in the apodosis of counterfactual conditionals in Middle and Early Modern English. An example is the sentence,

What would'st thou think of me, if I should weep. (p. 1723)

Although we could say that the form of *would'st* in this sentence is sub-junctive, to do so requires us to assume an analogical change. It may be preferable to be guided by morphology and say that the form *would'st* is indicative and hence that *would'st* is a true subjunctive substitute. Since the lexical meaning of the word serves the semantic function formerly served by the past subjunctive, we need not deny that the in-dicative mood has its usual signification.

In view of the morphological history of subjunctive substitute *would*, I see no reason not to analyze other modal auxiliaries in what once were contexts demanding the past subjunctive as past indicative in the modern language. The form of *could* then, in the sentence *He could do it if he tried,* is 'past indicative third singular'. Past tense signifies 'present or future and closed', while indicative mood signifies 'theoreti-cal'. Semantic and pragmatic information for the main clause is as follows:

pres/closed/theor (Can-prac (Do (he, it)) (he))

    pres - speaker
    closed - speaker
    theor - speaker
    prac - subject

The indicative mood signifies that the speaker intends the words to match the world, but the concept 'closed', conveyed by the past tense, qualifies the theoretical modality and shows that the speaker does not take the relation between words and world to be a holding relation. The clause represents the ability as an imagined possibility, but nonetheless in the theoretical modality.

Similarly the form *would*, in *It would rain if a wind came up,* is 'past indicative third singular'. Again, past tense signifies 'present or future and closed', while indicative mood signifies 'theoretical'. Semantic and pragmatic information for the main clause is as follows:

pres/closed/theor$_1$ (Will-theor$_2$ (Rain))

    pres - speaker
    closed - speaker
    theor$_1$ - speaker
    theor$_2$ - speaker

The verb stem *will* in this context has its theoretical sense because the state of affairs, 'its raining', cannot very well be intended. The semantic effect of *will* is to represent the state of affairs as a prospect. The effect of the past indicative is to represent this prospect as an imagined possibility. If the apodosis of this conditional sentence were *I would put on my jacket,* we could interpret *will* in its practical sense, in its theoretical sense, or as indeterminate, depending on whether we thought the speaker was expressing intention, prospectiveness, or intention-prospectiveness as an imagined possibility.

Since we can take the historically past subjunctive forms of the modal auxiliaries as past indicative forms without modifying our account of the semantics of the indicative, no obstacle remains to limiting the modern subjunctive to the present tense. We have no semantic reasons for not claiming that all past tense verbs, including modal auxiliaries, are past indicative verbs. So far, we have been able to maintain our traditional assumptions about the syntax of the English verb. We have been able to treat the modals as inflected for tense, mood, person, and number, although I have suggested that we need not treat them in this way. The question remains, though, whether we can treat the historically present tense forms of the modals as inflected. To do so we must be able to determine their mood.

A review of the distribution of present tense modals suggests that, with possibly one exception, all of them in all their uses can be analyzed as indicative. The possible exception is *may* in its use as a subjunctive substitute in independent clauses, as in the sentence,

     May God bless you.

The only formal indication, inversion of word order, suggests that *may* is subjunctive. Semantically, the clause clearly is not a representation that can be intended to match the world, and so the verb is apparently not indicative. To avoid claiming that *may* is an indicative, we can say that the word has a separate sense in this use and list that sense separately in the lexicon. This seems plausible since *may* in this use has virtually no semantic content aside from signifying practical modality. It does not seem to share any of the other senses that *may* has in other uses. The lexical entry for the word will state that it signifies 'practical modality' and is limited to independent clauses with inverted word order. We can then add 'May ＿＿＿＿＿ V$_{[main]}$ ＿＿＿＿＿' to our list of idioms in which the present subjunctive occurs. (We should also note that although we have called *may* a subjunctive substitute, it does not replace the subjunctive, for we are assuming that the subjunctive still occurs;

rather, *may* is a totally redundant reinforcing form.)

Although semantic evidence suggests that *may* in independent clauses expressing wish is subjective, there is no morphological evidence for this conclusion in present-day English. What little morphological evidence there is in Early Modern English (the period in which *may* becomes common in this use) suggests that *may* is indicative. The evidence comes from sentences with second person singular subjects like the following:

O mayst thou never dream of less delight. (p. 1786)

Unless we wish to consider such verbs in *-st* analogical subjunctives (a reasonable alternative, particularly in view of the use of verbs ending in *-est* or *-st* in counterfactual conditionals), we must call *mayst* in this sentence a present indicative. We then describe the sentence *O mayst thou dream,* which is identical in all relevant respects to the example at hand, as follows:

pres/theor (may-prac (Dream (thou)))

Calling *mayst* indicative poses a problem for the semantic analysis of that mood, for the sentence, despite falling intonation, does not make a statement. If we maintain that the indicative nonetheless signifies theoretical modality, we must explain how the modality is qualified so that the speaker is not interpreted as intending his words to match the world. To explain this we must appeal to context. Inversion shows that the sentence is not intended simply to state a fact, and the special sense of *may* in this use shows that the primary purpose of the sentence is to represent the state of affairs, 'thy dreaming' (or, in the original example, 'thy never dreaming of less delight'), as something to be brought about. The construction is perceived as an idiom, and the word *mayst* is not interpreted as an ordinary verb predicating a property of its subject. The theoretical modality signified by the indicative ending *-st*, being in conflict with the practical modality signified by the stem and not contributing intelligibly to the meaning of the sentence, is simply ignored. (Now we call *mayst* a true subjunctive substitute, a form which replaces the subjunctive and is not itself subjunctive.)

Other modals in independent clauses make statements and do not express wishes, as *may* in its special, idiomatic sense does. They can therefore be treated quite naturally as indicatives. This is fairly obvious in many cases, whether the modal is practical or theoretical. The sentence *He can do it* makes a statement about someone's present ability.

Semantically, the clause is as follows:

pres/theor (Can-prac (Do (he, it)) (he))

The sentence *It may rain* makes a statement about a present (theoretical) possibility. Semantically the clause is as follows:

pres/theor (May-theor (Rain))

Historically past tense forms which now signify simply 'present or future', not 'present or future and closed', can be treated in the same way. Thus *might* has a sense that is nearly synonymous with a sense of *may*. The sentence *It might rain* with *might* in this sense is semantically as follows:

pres/theor (Might-theor (Rain))

Might also has readings in which past tense retains a semantic function as in *It might be better if you went* or *It might be better to go,* in which past tense signifies 'present or future and closed'. Semantically, we have the following:

pres/closed/theor (May-theor (Better))

The state of affairs, 'its being better', is represented as an imagined possibility. A sentence like *It might rain* is sometimes interpreted as expressing an imagined possibility, with some condition like 'if a wind came up' being understood. But with no condition explicitly identified, the difference between imagined possibility and actual possibility is obscured, and *might* becomes a near equivalent of *may*. *Might* also has readings in which past tense signifies 'past', as in *They said it might rain,* used to report the statement, "It may rain." Semantically we have the following:

past/theor (May-theor (Rain))

The past tense maintains the sequence of tenses and is redundant with the past tense of *said*.

Sentences in which the morphological past tense signifies either 'past' or 'present or future and closed' we can generate with the rules we have already. The form of *might*, built on the stem *may*, is 'past indicative third singular'. Sentences in which the historical past tense retains no function require revision of the rules, but the revision can be accomplished easily at the lexical level. We simply add *might* as a verb stem belonging to the class of modal auxiliaries and define it in the lexicon. We explain the new sense as a development from an earlier sense in which *might* expressed imagined possibility. The form of *might* in this the new sense, the sense discussed with reference to the sentence *It might rain*, is then 'present indicative third singular'. Other historically past tense modals which can be reanalyzed as present tense forms in the modern language are *should, must,* and *ought*. Not all the modals have historically past tense forms which can be so analyzed, however. Neither *could* nor *would* has a sense in which past tense clearly signifies neither 'past' nor 'present or future and closed'. The new lexical rule needed to accommodate historically past tense forms which can now be interpreted as true presents is as follows:

(6d'') $V_{[aux][mod]}$ → {can, may, might, must, shall, should, will, ought, need, dare}

Each of the new stems *might, should,* and *ought* will be restricted to the present tense. The true past tense forms *might* and *should* will be generated as before from the stems *may* and *shall*. *Ought* apparently does not have a true past tense form any longer, since the historically past tense inflection -*t* seems never to signify either 'past' or 'present or future and closed'. I have therefore deleted the stem *ough-* from the list. The new present tense forms (we could call them the new preterite-presents) all make statements in independent clauses, suggesting that they, like the old present tense forms, should be treated as indicatives.

We have yet to encounter a present tense modal which we cannot analyze as indicative. Some potentially problematic cases remain, however, namely those in which the modal is used performatively. Examples are the following:

You may do it.
'I permit you to do it.'

Officers shall wear ties.
'I order officers to wear ties.'

She must be the president.
'I infer that she is the president.'

Boyd and Thorne (1969) treat the auxiliaries in these uses as having separate senses in which they convey such information as 'I permit', 'I order', and 'I infer'. Granting that it is possible to do so, it is more economical to treat the performative phenomenon as pragmatic, without adding new senses to the lexical definitions of the words. Each of the example sentences, the performative paraphrases notwithstanding, is a declarative sentence making a statement. The sentence *You may do it,* for instance, can be paraphrased, "You are permitted to do it," in which semantic and pragmatic information is as follows:

pres/theor (May-prac (Do (you, it)) (you))

> pres - speaker
> theor - speaker
> prac - subject: for the subject to bring about

We can treat the performative reading as semantically identical to the non-performative one. On both readings, the subject is said to have permission. On the performative reading, though, the speaker is interpreted as granting the permission. The state of affairs, 'your doing it', is therefore regarded as practical not only from the subject's point of view, but also from the speaker's, as in an imperative sentence. Pragmatic information for the performative reading is as follows:

> pres - speaker
> theor - speaker
> prac - speaker and subject: for the subject to bring about

The semantic content of the auxiliary verb *may* in the sense under consideration is comparable to the semantic content of the main verb *permit*. On the performative reading of the sentence *You may do it,* *may* is interpreted as *permit* is interpreted when its subject is 'I'. On the non-performative reading, *may* is interpreted as *permit* is interpreted when its subject is 'someone'. Even on its performative reading, the sentence makes a statement and can be true or false. If I say to someone, "You may do it," he could respond, "No I may not. You do not have the authority to permit me and the person who does has forbidden me." The person I have addressed has responded 'false' to my performative utterance of the sentence. As before in our analysis of the performative use of the verb *order,* we can maintain that in the performative use of *may* the speaker is assumed to be performing the action of permitting in describing the subject's being permitted. Very few of Boyd and Thorne's arguments are affected by this reanalysis, for we are only saying that they have described a combination of semantic and pragmatic information.

Our analysis of the performative uses of the modals shows that even in these uses the auxiliaries can be treated as indicative verbs. We have semantic reasons for calling the auxiliaries indicative, namely, that the sentences in question can be interpreted as statements. And historically they are also indicative. The form *shalt* in the sentence *Thou shalt not kill* is distinctively indicative, and the sentence has a performative use. Originally, such sentences also describe an obligation of the subject, just as sentences with *may* describe permission. If these sentences retained that function, the sentence *Officers shall wear ties* would be paraphrasable as "Officers have an obligation to wear ties." Semantic and pragmatic information would be as follows:

> pres/theor (shall-prac (Wear (officers, ties)) (officers))

> pres - speaker
> theor - speaker
> prac - subject: for the subject to bring about

On the performative reading, the state of affairs, 'officers' wearing ties', would be regarded as practical from the speaker's point of view as well as the subject's, and we would describe pragmatic information as follows:

> prac - speaker and subject: for the subject to bring about

It seems, however, that *shall* can no longer function as an ordinary predicate and can no longer describe an obligation of its subject. If I say, "Officers shall wear ties," and someone else responds, "No they shall not," the person responding cannot be interpreted as denying that officers have an obligation to wear ties and can only be interpreted as forbidding officers from wearing ties. Nor can the officers respond, "No we shall not. You don't have the authority to give the order." (In such a response, *shall* would not have the same sense that it has in the original utterance.) To reflect the semantic change in *shall,* we can describe the sentence *Officers shall wear ties* as follows:

> pres/theor (shall-prac (Wear (officers, ties)))

> pres - speaker
> theor - speaker

prac - speaker and subject: for the subject to bring about

The indicative mood of *shall* has come in conflict with the practical modality signified by the stem and is ignored. Although *shall* does not predicate obligation, it still refers the bringing about of the state of affairs represented in its complement to the subject, and in this respect is very much like the imperative mood.

In the only other environment in which the modals might be thought not to be indicative, we can find reasons for saying that they are. The environment in question is noun clauses after verbs which ordinarily govern the subjunctive. An example is the sentence,

> I also defend the right of any other free American citizen
> to demand that such an organisation shall not dictate his
> mode of thought. (p. 1622)

It is true that if the verb were not a modal auxiliary, it would be subjunctive, but since the auxiliary itself conveys the notion 'practical', the subjunctive would be redundant. Indeed, *shall* is used in such environments as a subjunctive substitute, and as in the other examples of substitution that we have observed, it can function as a full-fledged substitute because it makes the subjunctive semantically unnecessary. Furthermore, what little formal evidence there is suggests that the auxiliary verb is indicative. Consider the following sentences, adapted from the example above:

> He demands that the organisation shall not dictate thought.

> *He demands that the organisation not shall dictate thought.

> He demands that the organisation not dictate thought.

> *He demands that the organisation dictate not thought.

Note that the word *not* must follow the finite verb when the auxiliary *shall* is present but must precede the finite verb when the subjunctive mood is present, and so on syntactic grounds we can conclude that the verb *shall* in the noun clause of the first sentence is indicative, while the verb *dictate* in the noun clause of the third sentence is subjunctive. Taking *shall* as indicative, we describe the sentence *He demands that the organisation shall not dictate thought* schematically as follows:

pres₁/theor₁ (demand-prac₁ (pres₂/theor₂
(shall-prac₂ (not (dictate (organisation, thought))))) (he))

    pres₁ - speaker
    theor₁ - speaker
    prac₁ - one who demands (he)
    pres₂ - one who demands (he)
    theor₂ - one who demands (he)
    prac₂ - one who demands (he): redundant with prac₁

The theoretical modality signified by the indicative mood of *shall* (theor₂) and the practical modality signified by the stem itself (prac₂) are in conflict, with the result that the indicative mood is ignored. We can explain the conflict (and the way in which it is resolved) by observing that use of *shall* in this construction derives from the performative use of *shall* in independent clauses, and in this use *shall* originally predicates obligation of its subject. In the performative reading of the sentence *Thou shalt not dictate thought*, the practical modality signified by the stem of the verb is interpreted as reflecting not only the point of view of the subject (*thou*) but also the point of view of the speaker. The indicative mood signified by the ending is ignored because the speaker's purpose is recognized as being primarily to place an obligation on the subject, not to describe an obligation of the subject. For the sentence *He demands that the organisation shall not dictate thought*, we can say that a performative utterance has been reported in indirect speech and that the modality of the stem of *shall* (prac₂) reflects the original speaker's primary purpose, while the modality of the indicative ending (theor₂) reflects the original function of *shall* as a predicate used to describe an obligation, a function which is not required given the original speaker's primary purpose of imposing an obligation and which apparently has been completely lost in modern usage.

We have now shown that we can restrict the modern subjunctive to the present tense and, indeed, to the present tense of main verbs. The rules with which we began and a lexical description of the subjunctive which includes the necessary restrictions will generate finite main verbs. To account for the distribution of moods in the modal auxiliaries, we note that except for *may*, in a special sense occurring only in idiomatic independent clauses with inverted word order (and even here we do not have to treat *may* as an exception), all modals take the indicative. We also revise our rule describing the class of modal auxiliaries so that *might, must, should,* and *ought* are listed as stems that can be inflected for present tense. We have suggested that the new syntactic analysis restricting the subjunctive to the present tense is more realistic than the old analysis because formal criteria for distinguishing a past subjunctive have all but vanished, and semantic considerations do not force us to claim the existence of a past subjunctive. Because formal criteria for distinguishing a subjunctive from an imperative are minimal and because the two moods are semantically very similar, we may find it unrealistic to claim the existence of a present subjunctive as well. With minimal changes in our traditional assumptions, we can provide an analysis of English finite verbs which does not posit a subjunctive mood.

4.2.3 SEMANTIC DESCRIPTION OF THE MODERN SUBJUNCTIVE

Before undertaking the new analysis, let us summarize our results in a lexical description incorporating the assumptions of the preceding analysis. We have suggested that the subjunctive, because of its non-distinctiveness, has become increasingly restricted in the development from Old English to the present. Originally, the subjunctive signified only 'practical modality'. It still signifies practical modality, but it no longer co-occurs with the past tense nor with the modal auxiliaries, save *may* in idiomatic independent clauses. It no longer occurs in adverbial clauses, save literary conditional clauses. Its distribution in noun clauses has been sharply limited: it occurs only with words whose meanings exclude the concept 'theoretical' as semantically inappropriate. We might also note that many verbs which for semantic reasons exclude the indicative, verbs such as *wish* (expressing realizable wish), *want, desire,* and *order* do not usually take the subjunctive either. This is because they seldom take noun clause complements, though, not because of semantic incompatibility. A sentence like **I want that he come every day* is so awkward as to be unacceptable, the usual pattern being *I want him to come every day.* Yet a sentence like *?What I want is that he come every day* is much better and is perhaps marginally acceptable. Also, while the verbs *wish, desire,* and *order* generally take only infinitive complements, the corresponding nouns take noun clause complements more readily. Sentences like *?It is my wish (desire) that he come every day* are perhaps also marginally acceptable. As a result of being limited to occurring only with words that for semantic reasons exclude the indicative, the subjunctive in noun clauses now seems to be restricted to the complements of words which signify or can be interpreted as implying that the state of affairs that the complement represents is something for someone to bring about. The following semantic description, a proposed lexical entry for 'subjunctive', states these restrictions:

> subjunctive: occurs only with the PRESENT tense and with MAIN verbs or IDIOMATIC *MAY;* and is limited to IDIOMATIC INDEPENDENT CLAUSES (Long live _____, God save _____, Heaven help _____, Heaven forbid _____, God damn _____, Damn _____,..., May _____ V$_{[main]}$_____), to NOUN CLAUSES which are complements of words signifying or implying that the state of affairs represented is something FOR SOMEONE TO BRING ABOUT, and to CONDITIONAL CLAUSES which are LITERARY; and signifies that the clause represents a state of affairs in the PRACTICAL modality.

The restrictions will exclude the subjunctive from most of its earlier uses but allow it in the ones that remain. The restriction on the subjunctive in noun clauses will prevent it from occurring with the wide range of verbs that once allowed it.

4.2.4 ENGLISH WITHOUT A SUBJUNCTIVE MOOD

To analyze finite verbs without reference to a subjunctive mood, we must expand the domain of the imperative to include some of the subjunctive's uses and the domain of the indicative to include others. The indicative can easily absorb the subjunctive's use in conditional clauses. We simply list *be* as an alternant present indicative form and identify this form as 'literary'. The change causes no problems for semantic analysis since the indicative has long been the predominant mood in conditional clauses. (Indeed, we might wish to make this change even if we think it best to continue to posit a present subjunctive in the modern language.) The imperative can absorb the subjunctive's other two uses, but only if we allow it a degree of polysemy. The need to assume polysemy will detract somewhat from this reanalysis of the imperative.

The rationale for attempting the reanalysis is that the subjunctive and imperative have become phonologically identical and both signify practical modality. Furthermore, the imperative, in signifying that the state of affairs represented is something for the addressee to bring about, signifies volition on the part of the speaker and presupposes the enactability of the state of affairs represented by the clause. The subjunctive is now restricted to verbs signifying or implying volition, in that the state of affairs represented in their complements is something for someone to bring about, and the verbs also presuppose enactability, current enactability if they are present tense and earlier enactability if they are past tense. Since the subjunctive in noun clauses is now limited to environments in which 'volition' and its presupposition 'enactability' are present, we may wish to associate these notions with the form itself. Once we do this, the subjunctive in noun clauses is nearly identical semantically with the imperative. All that prevents a total identification of the two forms is the restriction on the imperative limiting it to 'vocative' subjects and the added signification that the state of affairs represented is for the subject to bring about. These differences are minimal and could be attributed to a polysemy in the imperative.

The subjunctive in independent clauses cannot be so easily assimilated to the imperative, however, for the semantic similarity between the two forms is only that they both signify practical modality. This is an important similarity, but the differences are important too, so much so that little is gained by attributing them to polysemy. We can treat the old subjunctive in independent clauses as an imperative if we like and claim that English now has only two moods, but the lexical entry for 'imperative' will list three separate senses, with the most general sense, 'practical modality', somewhat different from the other two and limited to idiomatic independent clauses. We would then have two uses of the imperative in independent clauses and a 'polysemy' that approaches more radical kinds of ambiguity. We would therefore have little reason not to list the mood occurring in idiomatic independent clauses separately in the lexicon and call it by its old name.

4.2.5 CHOOSING AMONG ALTERNATIVES

In describing the syntax of the present-day English moods, I have made little effort to evaluate alternative analyses, as I have no way to make an exact measure of their advantages and disadvantages. Even so, we can make general observations about what will affect our choice. Obviously, the analysis we choose must suit our purposes. If our purpose is to describe the modern language in historical perspective, the best analysis is probably the traditional one in which finite verbs can have any of three moods and in which the subjunctive can be present or past. This analysis reflects the historical continuity of the language, and it remains plausible, for the old inflectional forms can still be identified on formal criteria.

Any reanalysis assumes a change in the system which the traditional analysis describes. We do have reason to assume some change, but reanalyses which assume the least change will be most plausible from a diachronic point of view. We have two reasons, it seems to me, to seek a reanalysis of finite verbs. One is that inflectional categories are so seldom distinctive. The other is that modern speakers unschooled in grammar seem unaware of a system of three moods. They seem aware of a system of two tenses and associate the forms of the verbs in sentences like *It is so* and *It was so* as differing in only one element, even if they do not know the grammarian's name for that element. But they do not seem aware of a system of moods which distinguishes a subjunctive mood from an indicative mood. They do not seem aware that the forms of the verbs in the pairs of clauses *that it be so* and *that it is so* and *if it were so* and *if it was so* differ in one and the same element, nor do they associate the forms of verbs in the clauses *if it be so* and *if it were so* as being different in one element, tense, but the same in another element, mood. They do seem aware of a system which distinguishes the forms of verbs in the noun clauses *They insist that you be early* and *They insist that you are early,* but I presume that they would be as likely to associate this difference with the difference in the forms of the verbs in the sentences *Be early* and *You are early* as to recognize a three-way distinction in form. With these two considerations in mind, morphological form and speakers' intuitions about morphological form, I have outlined new ways of analyzing finite verbs.

The alternative I prefer combines features of some of the reanalyses I have proposed. I think that the most realistic assumption, from a psychological point of view, is that English has two fully productive moods, an indicative and an imperative. I would call the historically present subjunctive forms in conditional clauses 'literary' present indicative forms and the historically past subjunctive forms in conditional clauses past indicative forms, with first and third person singular *were* marked 'literary' or 'educated'. I would call the historically present subjunctive in noun clauses an imperative, acknowledging a degree of polysemy in that mood: the imperative has special restrictions when it occurs in independent clauses. I would treat the historically present subjunctive form in independent clauses as a special mood confined to idioms. I would treat it as a single mood signifying practical modality, but as multiply polysemous, having separate senses in its separate idioms. My reasons for doing this would be that I do not believe that modern speakers associate the forms of the verbs in the sentences *Long live the queen, Praise be to God, Bless you,* and *Damn it.*

My choice of alternatives, based partly on morphology but largely on my impression of how speakers interpret the forms, is admittedly subjective, but the grammarian must decide how he is going to analyze the forms of the language he is studying, and if he cannot choose an alternative from several possibilities using purely objective criteria, he must choose the one that strikes him as most plausible. For me to argue further for the alternative I prefer would serve no purpose. My primary objective has been to propose a semantic description of the form traditionally called the subjunctive, and while it would be desirable to identify the role of that form in the current syntactic system of the language, it is not ultimately necessary. Indeed in discussing alternative analyses, I hope to have shown that semantic descriptions of the subjunctive which make 'practical modality' an essential feature are compatible with a variety of syntactic descriptions and therefore compatible with historical change. To propose a syntactic description of the subjunctive and argue persuasively for it would involve issues in syntactic theory that are quite separate from the semantic issues I have set out to address.

4.3 SUMMARY

The historical trend of declining use may require us to list new restrictions in our semantic description of the subjunctive but not to revise our statement that it signifies practical modality. Describing the semantics of the mood in the way we have done helps to explain how other modal forms have come to substitute for it: in contexts in which modality is important, words signifying the same modality, particularly *may, shall,* and *will,* first reinforce and then replace the non-distinctive subjunctive. These words have undergone semantic changes, and they do not always continue to signify practical modality in present-day English, but these changes too can be explained within the theory of two modalities. Use of the subjunctive has declined so much that we may be led to assume changes in the syntax and morphology of finite verbs, but no matter how we revise our syntactic descriptions we can retain the key element of our semantic description. To the extent that the subjunctive remains, it continues to signify practical modality, as it always did. If we assume that no subjunctive remains, we can still maintain that the old subjunctive verbs in idiomatic independent clauses convey practical modality, however we choose to identify the source of the modality, and we can maintain that the old subjunctive verbs in noun clauses are now imperative verbs, the imperative being another practical mood. In short, the hypothesis that the subjunctive signifies practical modality is consistent with earlier uses of the mood and with historical changes that have sharply limited its use.

5

EXTENSIONS AND CONCLUSIONS

Our hypothesis about the subjunctive's signification has allowed us to account for the mood's distribution in a unified way, both in modern times and in earlier times, when the subjunctive was far more frequent. It has also allowed us to see semantic connections between the subjunctive and other modal forms in English. The hypothesis is formulated within a very general theory about manner of representation, so we would expect to be able to design similar semantic descriptions for modal forms in other languages, descriptions which are compatible with the distribution of the forms. In this section I briefly examine modal inflections in Modern French and Classical Attic Greek which are semantically comparable to the English subjunctive. The results will suggest that the theory of two modalities can be applied to modal forms in other languages.

5.1 FRENCH MOODS

People who speak both French and English notice striking similarities and striking differences in the distribution of the moods called 'subjunctive' in those languages. Here, without attempting a full analysis of the French subjunctive, I will suggest that it is a practical mood, contrasting with a theoretical mood, the indicative, another practical mood, the imperative, and a theoretical (or indeterminate) mood, originally a periphrastic containing a practical modal, the conditional.

Initial reason for taking the French subjunctive to be a practical mood is the meaning it has in independent clauses. It occurs, much as the English subjunctive does, in idiomatic sentences such as the following:[26]

> Vive la République.
> 'Long live the Republic.'

> Dieu vous bénisse.
> 'God bless you.'

> Qui m'aime me suive.
> 'Let him who loves me follow me.'

In such expressions of wish and exhortation, the state of affairs represented is something to be brought about, not something to be perceived. Similarly, in more productive uses, in clauses introduced by *que* 'that', the subjunctive signifies practical modality, as in the sentence,

> Qu'elle soit heureuse!
> 'May she be happy!'

In dependent clauses the subjunctive occurs in the complements of words which themselves signify practical modality, such as *vouloir* 'want', *désirer* 'wish', *souhaiter* 'wish', *exiger* 'demand', and *demander* 'request'. Examples are the sentences,

> Elle veut que vous l'accompagniez.
> 'She wants you to accompany her.'

> J'exige qu'il soit puni.
> 'I demand that he be punished.'

Such uses of the French subjunctive in independent and dependent clauses correspond to surviving uses of the English subjunctive, and manner of representation is clearly practical.

The French subjunctive has a much wider distribution than the English subjunctive and frequently occurs where English uses the indicative. One such case is in the complements of words expressing emotion, as in the sentence,

Je suis content que vous soyez ici.
'I am glad you are here.'

Although the French adjective *content* presupposes the state of affairs represented in its complement as fact, just as the English adjective *glad* does, we can still maintain that the French subjunctive signifies practical modality. French *content* also conveys the notion 'desirability', a concept involving representation in the practical manner, and this makes the subjunctive appropriate. French *content* and English *glad* have features of meaning that make both a practical and a theoretical mood appropriate but in both languages only one mood can occur at a time. In French, the subjunctive is chosen for one reason; in English, the indicative is chosen for another.

Another case in which distribution of the subjunctive differs is in the complements of words expressing belief. Present-day English requires the indicative, but earlier English had irregular variation. Modern French has variation, but the variation is systematic. Verbs of believing in positive clauses take the indicative, but in negative clauses, the subjunctive, unless the speaker wishes to express certainty. An example with the subjunctive is the sentence,

Je ne crois pas que ce livre soit interéssant.
'I don't think this book is interesting.'

Factors that make the subjunctive appropriate with verbs of believing in earlier English, I have suggested, are that 'belief' may be accompanied by an emotional attitude such as hope or fear, that 'belief' may involve uncertainty, and that when the subject of the verb of believing is second or third person, the points of view of subject and speaker may differ. Some or all of these factors may once have played a role in French. Since the verbs themselves express theoretical modality and since the subject of the verb indicates the point of view from which the state of affairs is represented as something to be perceived, mood is not of crucial importance. Because belief is compatible with desire, practical modality in the complement does not necessarily conflict with theoretical modality in the verb. Furthermore, verbs of believing qualify modality and so does negation. By choosing the subjunctive, the speaker reinforces the qualifying effects of the verb and of negation; he chooses a mood which does not allow the hearer to interpret either him or the subject as taking the words as actually matching the world. Use of the French subjunctive with verbs signifying theoretical modality does not require us to analyze the subjunctive in this use as a theoretical mood since reasons for using a practical mood in this context can be found. If the subjunctive does not appear to mean what it means in independent clauses, we can explain the difference as a result of the effects of context.

The subjunctive has other uses in French, and its range is in fact quite similar to the English subjunctive's earlier range. It occurs in noun clauses after impersonal verbs expressing necessity, compulsion, suitability, possibility, doubt, and emotion, and it occurs in adverbial clauses after conjunctions expressing purpose, time limit, and concession. In some of these uses modality is clearly practical. In others, modality may seem doubtful since a theoretical mood would seem equally appropriate, but the doubtful cases do not entail that the subjunctive does not or does not always signify practical modality. In French, as in English, mood is obligatory, and one mood or another must be chosen, whether it is fully appropriate or not. That the notion 'practical' is obscured in some uses is again attributable to context.

The French indicative and imperative are sufficiently like the English indicative and imperative semantically that I will assume without further argument that they can be described in accordance with the theory of two modalities. The indicative signifies theoretical modality and nothing else. The imperative signifies practical modality and that the state of affairs represented is for the addressee to bring about. It is also syntactically restricted, as is the English imperative, though it allows first person plural subjects.

The French conditional mood is remarkably like the English periphrastic construction of *would* (or *should*) and the infinitive. Historically, it too is a periphrastic, composed of an infinitive plus the finite auxiliary *habere* 'have' in the imperfect indicative. The Latin phrase *cantare habebam* 'to sing I was having' ('I had to sing') becomes Modern French *(je) chanterais* 'I would (should) sing'. The morphological connection between the conditional endings and the imperfect indicative of the verb *avoir* 'have' is still apparent. The semantic connection is no longer apparent, but presumably the following changes took place: *habere* in Latin has the basic meaning 'have, hold'; it develops a weakened sense 'obliged' (compare English *I have a song, I have a song to sing, I have to sing a song, I have to sing*), which sense implies 'prospectiveness' and 'futurity'. With a form signifying past time, like the imperfect, the word signifies either a past obligation or a past prospect, and no doubt is often indeterminate between the two. The development is parallel with the development of English *shall*. Latin *cantare habeo,* with present indicative *habeo,* first means 'I have to sing', then 'I shall sing'; Latin *cantare habebam,* with imperfect indicative *habebam,* first means 'I was having to sing', then 'I should sing'.

The indeterminacy of the modal *habere* makes it impossible to be certain of an exact sequence in the semantic development. Even in Latin, *habere* has occurrences in which only prospectiveness, and not also obligation, is meant. The sense 'obliged' must have preceded the sense 'prospective', but by the time the verb becomes a conditional ending, we cannot tell whether modality is practical or theoretical; we cannot tell whether the form conveys a notion of compulsion and so represents a state of affairs as a past necessity, or whether it conveys only prospectiveness and so represents a state of affairs as a past prospect. I assume that the Modern French conditional signifies theoretical modality because the auxiliary *habere* is inflectionally indicative originally, and once it loses its earlier sense 'obligation', no form conveying practical modality remains. Also, the accompanying conditional clause in Modern French has its verb in the imperfect indicative, which I assume signifies theoretical modality, and I see no reason to assume that manner of representation in the two clauses is different. Making the semantic development even harder to trace is that *habere* has another closely related sense, 'have in mind, intend', and the French future and conditional forms could just as well have developed from this sense, with the forms paralleling the semantic development of *will*. In any case, the notion 'past' conveyed by the imperfect makes the question of correspondence between words and world closed, whether the auxiliary is interpreted as signifying 'past and necessary (intended)', 'past and prospective', or 'past and necessary-prospective (intended-prospective)'. *Habere,* being forward-looking, has the same effect on the imperfect as the English subjunctive has on the past tense, causing its implication 'closed' to replace its earlier meaning.

Although French has four moods and English only three (perhaps two), the modal systems are quite similar semantically. Our theory of two modalities allows us to describe what the moods of the different languages signify in a way that reflects semantic similarities but is consistent with differences in distribution. Our theory also helps to account for historical change in French. The conditional mood replaces the Latin imperfect subjunctive as a form expressing 'imagined possibility'. The Latin subjunctive, a practical mood like the English subjunctive, produces the notion 'imagined possibility' when combined with the imperfect just as the English subjunctive does when combined with the past tense. The process of replacement, in which one originally practical modal substitutes for another, closely parallels the same process in English, in which the auxiliaries *should* and *would* substitute for the past subjunctive. The indeterminacy of the French conditional in the early stages of its development (or perhaps even now), like the frequent indeterminacy of English *should* and *would,* does not refute the hypothesis of two modalities. Indeterminacy can be explained historically with reference to an implication of the practical modal *habere,* and it can be explained pragmatically with reference to the communicative purpose of a hypothetical statement, which is to represent an imagined possibility, and not to get words to match world nor world to match words. We can conclude that the French moods confirm our expectation that our theory of two modalities has applications beyond English. The Greek moods will provide further confirmation.

5.2 GREEK MOODS

Classical Attic Greek has four moods: indicative, imperative, subjunctive, and optative. The indicative and imperative are semantically sufficiently like the corresponding moods in English and French that I will again assume without argument that they can be described in accordance with our theory of modality. The Greek subjunctive, cognate with the French subjunctive, and the Greek optative, cognate with the English 'subjunctive', are semantically similar, and both apparently are practical moods. Differentiating these two moods semantically is a difficult problem, long debated among Indo-Europeanists. Here I will only suggest that our theory of modality is consistent with the data and can be used to some avail in a close analysis.

Evidence that both the subjunctive and optative are practical moods is their use in independent clauses. The subjunctive mood in a very typical use (the so-called hortatory subjunctive) is closely akin to the imperative and is often said to compensate for the lack of a first person imperative. An example is the sentence,[27]

μήπω ἐκεῖσε ἴωμεν.
'Let's not go there yet.'

The notions 'volition' and 'prospectiveness' combine in this use. In other uses, one of these two notions can be emphasized, almost to the exclusion of the other. The optative mood in a very typical use expresses realizable wish, as in the sentence,

ἐξολοίμην.
'May I perish.'

And in a very typical use with the qualifying particle ἄν (the so-called potential optative), the mood expresses imagined possibility, as in the sentence,

ἅπαντες ἄν ὁμολογήσειαν.
'All would agree.'

The notions 'desire', 'potential', and 'prospectiveness' combine in these two uses, receiving varying degrees of emphasis. While both moods signify practical modality, the subjunctive appears to be more specific: perhaps it signifies 'practical modality' and 'open possibility', while the optative signifies only 'practical modality'. Signifying 'open possibility', the subjunctive would always imply future time. Not containing 'open possibility' as part of its signification, the optative would be capable of expressing either open or closed possibility. Both the subjunctive and the optative occur in a wide range of dependent clauses, including purpose clauses and clauses after verbs of fearing and in indirect discourse. The subjunctive occurs after clauses with a main verb in one of the 'primary tenses' (present, future, perfect, future perfect), and the optative, after clauses with a main verb in one of the 'secondary tenses' (imperfect, aorist, pluperfect), again suggesting that the notion 'open possibility', with an implication 'future' when combined with practical modality, is part of the signification of the subjunctive. Further, the subjunctive occurs in conditional clauses expressing condition which is actually possible, and the optative, in conditional clauses expressing condition which is not necessarily actually possible.

   The optative is not used to express condition which is necessarily not actually possible (condition which is definitely contrary to fact, not just possibly contrary to fact). Although the optative in earlier Homeric Greek could have this use, in Classical Attic Greek only the indicative will serve. The pattern of formation is as follows: for present time, the protasis has εἰ + the imperfect indicative, and the apodosis has the imperfect indicative + ἄν; for past time, the protasis has εἰ + the aorist indicative, and the apodosis has the aorist indicative + ἄν. Attic Greek distinguishes formally between what I have earlier called the less restrictive kind of closed possibility, for which the question of correspondence is not conceived as open, and the more restrictive kind, for which the question is conceived as not open, using the optative for the former and the indicative for the latter. The indicative's occurrence in these constructions in Greek by no means entails that this mood is semantically unlike the English indicative. The Greek and English indicative share many common uses (most notably, both express facts in declarative sentences), and historically they are cognate, so we have no reason to assume that the Greek indicative signifies anything other than the theoretical modality. The Greek constructions for expressing counterfactual condition and idle wish are functionally equivalent to the English constructions in the past subjunctive since they serve the same communicative purposes, but they are not semantically identical. Rather, the Greek constructions are semantically more akin to the English sequences mentioned above (Section 4.2.1) that begin ''Imagine a world'' or ''Suppose this, which we know is not true'' and continue with the indicative. The particle ἄν in the apodosis qualifies the theoretical modality signified by the indicative mood of the verbs in both clauses by conveying the notion 'imagined', just as the explicit, though inefficient, introductory expressions *Imagine a world* and *Suppose this, which we know is not true* qualify the theoretical modality signified by the indicative mood of all the verbs that may follow.

The Greek moods provide an interesting contrast to the English moods. Greek has more moods and distributes them quite differently, yet a cursory survey suggests that the theory of modality will apply in Greek too. Describing the imperative, the subjunctive, and the optative all as signifying 'practical' is plausible, given their uses in independent clauses, and distinguishing them from each other with additional semantic features and syntactic restrictions would seem a promising approach. Pragmatic information will also play an important role in explaining the meanings the moods acquire in particular uses. The somewhat startling use of the indicative in certain kinds of hypothetical statements can also be explained without assuming ambiguity or otherwise preventing a unified account of the uses of that mood. Like French moods, Greek moods also seem to show that the theory has applications beyond English and facilitates comparison of moods in different languages.

5.3 CONCLUSIONS

The hypothesis that the English subjunctive signifies practical modality is consistent with current and earlier uses of the present and past subjunctive. The hypothesis helps to explain the process by which other forms come to replace this mood as it becomes phonologically nondistinctive, and the hypothesis is unaffected by considerations of syntactic change, however we choose to describe such change. Our semantic analysis of the subjunctive, carried out within a general theory of modality, facilitates comparison with other moods and with other modal forms in English. The theory of modality, based on a fundamental distinction between two separate manners of representation, should apply to all languages and should facilitate comparisons between languages, as the brief analysis of moods in French and Greek shows. By clarifying the notion 'manner of representation' and hence the kind of semantic information that modal forms convey, the theory solves problems in the analysis of English moods and will doubtless prove useful in answering other questions about modality in English and other languages.

APPENDIX A

INFLECTION OF OLD ENGLISH VERBS

Strong Verbs: e.g., rīdan 'ride'

	Indicative	Subjunctive	Imperative
Present			
Sg. 1.	rīde	rīde	
2.	rītst	rīde	rīd
3.	rītt	rīde	
Pl. 1.	rīdaþ	rīden	
2.	rīdaþ	rīden	rīdaþ
3.	rīdaþ	rīden	
Past			
Sg. 1.	rād	ride	
2.	ride	ride	
3.	rād	ride	
Pl. 1.	ridon	riden	
2.	ridon	riden	
3.	ridon	riden	

Infinitive:	rīdan, tō rīdenne
Present participle:	rīdende
Past participle:	riden

Weak Verbs: e.g., *fremman* 'do'

	Indicative	Subjunctive	Imperative
Present			
Sg. 1.	fremme	fremme	
2.	fremst	fremme	freme
3.	fremþ	fremme	
Pl. 1.	fremmaþ	fremmen	
2.	fremmaþ	fremmen	fremmaþ
3.	fremmaþ	fremmen	
Past			
Sg. 1.	fremede	fremede	
2.	fremedest	fremede	
3.	fremede	fremede	
Pl. 1.	fremedon	fremeden	
2.	fremedon	fremeden	
3.	fremedon	fremeden	

Infinitive:	fremman, tō fremmenne
Present participle:	fremmende
Past participle:	fremed

Preterite-Present Verbs: e.g., *sculan* 'shall'

	Indicative	Subjunctive
Present		
Sg. 1.	sceal	scyle
2.	scealt	scyle
3.	sceal	scyle
Pl. 1.	sculon	scylen
2.	sculon	scylen
3.	sculon	scylen
Past		
Sg. 1.	sceolde	sceolde
2.	sceoldest	sceolde
3.	sceolde	sceolde
Pl. 1.	sceoldon	sceolden
2.	sceoldon	sceolden
3.	sceoldon	sceolden

Infinitive:	sculan

Anomalous Verbs: e.g., *bēon* 'be'

	Indicative	*Subjunctive*	*Imperative*
Present			
Sg. 1.	eom, bēo	sīe, bēo	
2.	eart, bist	sīe, bēo	bēo
3.	is, biþ	sīe, bēo	
Pl. 1.	sindon, sint	sīen, bēon	
2.	sindon, sint	sīen, bēon	bēoþ
3.	sindon, sint	sīen, bēon	
Past			
Sg. 1.	wæs	wǣre	
2.	wǣre	wǣre	
3.	wæs	wǣre	
Pl. 1.	wǣron	wǣren	
2.	wǣron	wǣren	
3.	wǣron	wǣren	

Infinitive:	bēon, tō bēonne
Present Participle:	bēonde

APPENDIX B

CITATIONS

This appendix reproduces all the citations from F. Th. Visser's *An Historical Syntax of the English Language* which appear in the text. Beneath each citation is the sentence and its immediate context as it occurs in the primary source. Citations are listed in the order of Visser's page numbers. Full bibliographic references for primary sources are given at the end of the appendix. (Note that I have not always been able to obtain the same edition that Visser cites.)

Page	Citation
698	a man must endeavour to look wholesome, lest he makes so nauseous a figure in the side-bax.
	nat that I pretend to be a Beau; but a man must endeavour to look wholesome, lest he makes so nauseous a Figure in the Side-bax, the Ladies shou'd be compell'd to turn their Eyes upon the Play. (Vanbrugh, II.i)
796	Geweorðe me æfter þinum worde.
	Ða cwæþ Maria, "Her is Drihtnes þinen; geweorðe me æfter ðinum worde." And se engel hyre framgewat. (Bosworth, Luke I, 38)
797	Be this sweet Helen's knell.

Our own love waking cries to see what's done,
While shameful hate sleeps out the afternoon.
Be this sweet Helen's knell, and now forget her.
(Shakespeare, All's Well, V.iii.65-67)

813   It were time we left our wine flagons.

"Conclamatum est, poculatum est," said Prior Aymer:
"we have drunk and we have shouted, — it were time
we left our wine flagons."
(Scott, Ch. XIV)

813   'Twere baseness to deny my love.

I know 'twas Madness to declare this Truth.
And yet 'twere Baseness to deny my Love.
(Dryden, I.i)

816   Should I not play may part, I were too blame.

Porcia: Make all the haste you can, pray Flora.
Flora: Madam, I'll flie. Should I not play my part,
       I were too blame,
       Since all my Fortune's betted on her Game.
(Tuke, I.i)

816   gif þu wære her, nære min broðor dead.

Ða cwæð Martha to þam Hælende: Dryhten, gif þu
wære her, nære min broþor dead.
(Thorpe, John 11, 21)

829   he bad, that thider were brought the quen.

But or bad he, þat þider were brouht þe quen, . . .
(Lay of Havelock, l. 2392-93)

842—843   I thought upon Antonio when he told me, and
               wished in silence that it were not his.

Salerio: I thought upon Anthonio when he told me,
         and wisht in silence that it were not his.
(Shakespeare, Merchant, II.viii.31-32)

843   he wishes all we are told be true.

We four sat down presently to our business, and in an
hour despatched all our talk; and did inform Sir
Thomas Allen well in it, who, I perceive, in serious
matters, is a serious man: and tells me he wishes all we
are told be true, in our defence.
                                                    (Braybrooke)

850   I hope he be in love.

Bene. Gallants, I am not as I haue bin.
Leo. So say I, me thinkes you are sadder.
Claud. I hope he be in loue.
            (Shakespeare, Much Ado, III.ii.15-17)

851   Y trowe thy knyfe be gode y-nogh.

"Syr Awntour," seyde the kynge, "thou hym slowe,
Y trowe thy knyfe be gode y-nogh,
Gyf that thy wylle bee."
                        (Halliwell, "Sir Eglamour")

853   heo ... cwæð þæt heo wære wydewe.

                            ... þæt heo hi geneosode
and ongan hyre sæcgan hyre sweartan geþohtas
cwæð þæt heo wære wydewe on þam geare ...
            (Ælfric's Lives II, "Saint Eugenia")

854   he segð, þæt he si Crist cyning.

and forbeodende þæt man þam Casere gafol ne sealde,
and segð þæt he sig Crist Cyning.
                            (Thorpe, Luke 23, 2)

857   Now aske of me what it be.

Menstrel, me likeþ wel þi gle
Now aske of me what it be, Largelich ichil þe pay:
Now speke, & tow migt asay.
                            (Sir Orfeo, 1. 450)

857   Know of the duke, if his last purpose hold.

Know of the Duke if his last purpose hold,
Or whether since he is advis'd by ought
To change the course, hee's full of alteration
And selfe reproving, bring his constant pleasure.
         (Shakespeare, King Lear, V.i.1 – 4)

863   ic com . . . þ he wære geswutelud.

And ic hyne nyste: ac ic com and fullode on wætere,
to þam þæt he wære geswutelod on Israhela folce.
         (Thorpe, John 1, 31)

864   Doubt not byt I will use my utmost skill,
           So that the Pope attend to your complaint.

Doubt not but I will use my utmost skill,
So that the Pope attend to your complaint.
         (Shelley, I.ii)

872   they will forget before the week be out.

While others are filling their memory with a lumber of
words, one-half of which they will forget before the
week be out, your truant may learn some really useful
art.
         (Stevenson)

876   there was nothing more to be said till Sir
           Thomas were present.

There was nothing more to be said, or that could be
said to any purpose, till Sir Thomas were present.
         (Austen, II, 5)

900   How much wouldst thou, hadst thou thy Senses, say to
           each of us.

When does my heart so little obey my reason as to la-
ment thee, thou excellent man! — Heaven receive him,
or restore him! — Thy beloved mother, thy obliged

friends, thy helpless servants, stand around thee without distinction. How much wouldst thou, hadst thou thy senses, say to each of us!

(Spectator, 215)

900   was I now to disappoint the young creature, her
           death would be the consequence.

... I am well satisfied, that, was I now to disappoint the young creature, her death would be the consequence, and I should look upon myself as her murderer.

(Fielding, XIV, ix)

904   this same Cassio, though he speak of comfort, ...
           yet he looks sadly.

But this same Cassio, tho he speake of comfort, Touching the Turkish loss, yet he lookes sadly.

(Shakespeare, Othello, II.i.31–32)

904   For though Christ were beleved and taught,
           yet the multitude eftsones grewe to a shameles
           kinde of libertie.

for though Christ were beleeved and taught, yet the multitude eft soone, grew to a shamelesse kinde of liberty, making no more of necessary points of Doctrine, then served their loose humour.

(Campion, II, I)

905   Christmas morning though it be, it is necessary
           to sent up workmen.

Christmas morning though it be, it is necessary to send up workmen, to ascertain the extent of the damage done.

(Dickens)

905   if you loved me as I wish, though I were an
           Æthiop, you'd think none so fair.

Now this is not well from you, Julia—I despise person
in a man—yet if you loved me as I wish, though I were
an Æthiop, you'd think none so fair.
(Sheridan, III.ii)

905   Though he were dying, he assured himself, he
would not send for him.

[Primary source not available]
(Garvice)

905   He that smiteth a man so that he die, shall
be surely put to death.

He that smiteth a man, so that he die, shall be
surely put to death.
(Holy Bible, Ex. 21, 12)

931   do it so cunningly That my discovery be not
aimed at.

But, good my lord, do it so cunningly,
That my discov'ry be not aimed at.
(Shakespeare, Two Gentlemen, III.i.44–45)

1622   The memorial asks that Parliament shall make it
illegal to vivisect dogs.

[Primary source not available]
(Westminster Gazette, no. 8080, 21)

1622   I also defend the right of any other free American
citizen to demand that such an organisation shall
not dictate his mode of thought.

Regarding religious, political, and social organizations,
I defend the right of every man in our free America to
organize with his fellows when and as he pleases, for
any purpose he pleases, but I also defend the right of
any other free American citizen to demand that such an
organization shall not dictate his mode of thought or, so
long as it be moral, his mode of conduct.
(Lewis)

150

1641   I . . . rēsolved, if His Highness did come again, he
            should see me under no disadvantages.

            Now I began to understand him, and resolv'd, if his
            Highness did come again, he should see me under no
            Disadvantages, if I could help it: I told him, if *his
            Highness* did me the Honour to see me again, I hop'd
            he would not let me be so surpriz'd as I was before.
                                                        (Defoe)

1655   Moyses us bebead on þærc æ þæt we sceoldon
            þus gerade mid stanum oftorfian (mandabit
            nobis huius modi lapidare).

            Moyses us bebead, on þære æ, þæt we sceoldon þus
            gerade mid stanum oftorfian: hwæt cwyst þu?
                                            (Thorpe, John 8, 5–6)

1656   He . . . requested that a bowl of Devonshire cream
            should be passed along.

            Lord Garvington made no reply, as breakfast, in his
            opinion, was much too serious a business to be inter-
            rupted. He reached for the marmalade, and requested
            that a bowl of Devonshire cream should be passed
            along.
                                                        (Hume)

1695   I desire that you will do no such thing.

            "I desire that you will do no such thing," said the
            bishop, now again looking up at her. "You may be
            sure that I shall," said Mrs. Proudie . . .
                                            (Trollope, II, 66)

1709   She . . . faltered out her command that he would
            sit down.

            She observed that Tenison had been long standing at
            her bedside, and with that sweet courtesy which was
            habitual to her, faltered out her commands that he
            would sit down, and repeated them till he obeyed.
                                            (Macaulay, T., XX)

1723   What would'st thou think of me, if I should weep?

"What wouldst thou thinke of me if I should weep?"
"I woulde thincke thee a most princely hypocrite."
(Shakespeare, Henry IV, II.ii.56)

1732   if I'd of known . . . , I'd have gone after supper.

But if I'd of known you were all going to get home
so prompt, I'd have gone after supper instead.
(Macaulay, R., VII)

1733   I wish the snow would melt.

I wish the snow would melt and the sun come out on high:
I long to see a flower so before the day I die.
(Tennyson, "The May Queen")

1782   whisper softly that he may not heare.

Pray whisper softly that he may not heare,
Or else such words as shall not blast his eare.
(Davenant, Epilogue 7–8)

1782   I made the groom ride him, that you might
see him.

He is outside: I made the groom ride him, that you
might see him. He had the side-saddle on for an hour or
two yesterday. Come to the window and look at him.
(Eliot, III, 27)

1784   I wish my patience may be strong enough.

How beautifull is sorrow when it dwells
Within these Ladies eyes? so comely, that it makes
Felicity in others seeme deform'd.
I wish my patience may be strong enough.
(Davenant, 32)

1785   I fear it may lead to nothing.

P.S. Have just opened this letter again after a turn round the garden, during which I made a somewhat strange discovery. I fear it may lead to nothing more interesting than some pretty yokel idyll.

(Allingham)

1786　　　　　O mayst thou never dream of less delight.

O mayst thou never dream of less delight,
Nor ever wake to less substantial joys!
(Congreve, V.iii)

1796　　　　　so mote God make your ofspring . . . remember you.

Remember our thyrst whyle ye sit & drink: our hounger whyle ye be feastynge: our restles watche whyle ye be slepyng: our sore and grieuous payne whyle ye be playing: our hote burning fyre while ye bee in pleasure and sportynge: so mote God make your ofspryng after remember you: so Gode kepe you hence, or not long here, but bring you shortely to that blisse, to which for our lordes loue helpe you to bring us, and we shal set hand to helpe you thether to us.

(More)

REFERENCES FOR PRIMARY SOURCES

Ælfric's Lives of Saints. Part I. Ed. Walter W. Skeat. Early English Text Society. London: N. Trubner, 1881. 34 – 35.

Allingham, Margery. *Dancers in Mourning*. New York, 1937; rpt. New York: Bantam, 1984. 150.

Austen, Jane. *Mansfield Park: A Novel*. Vol. 2. London: T. Egerton, 1814. 93 – 94.

Bosworth, Joseph, ed. *The Gospels: Gothic, Anglo-Saxon, Wycliffe and Tyndale Versions*. 4th ed. London: Gibbings & Co., 1907. 272.

Braybrooke, Richard Lord, ed. *Diary and Correspondence of Samuel Pepys, F.R.S.* Vol. 3. London: George Allen & Unwin, 1848. 484.

Campion, Edmund. *The History of Ireland. Two Histories of Ireland*. Dublin: Society of Stationers, 1633. II,i,55 – 56.

Congreve, William. "The Mourning Bride." Havelock Ellis, ed. *The Best Plays of the Old Dramatists: William Congreve*. Mermaid Series. London: Vizetelly, 1887. V.iii.

Davenant, W. *Love and Honour*. London: Hum, Robinson, and Moseley, 1649. 32 and Epilogue 7 – 8.

Defoe, Daniel. *Roxana*. Ed. Jane Jack. London: Oxford University Press, 1964. 60 – 61.

Dickens, Charles. *The Mystery of Edwin Drood*. London: Chapman & Hall, 1870. 114.

Dryden, John. *The Spanish Fryar or, The Double Discovery*. London: Richard Tonson, 1681. I.i.

Eliot, George. *Daniel Deronda*. Vol. 1. New York: Mershon, n.d. 273.

Fielding, Henry. *The History of Tom Jones a Foundling*. New York: Modern Library, 1930. 686.

Garvice, Charles. *Staunch as a Woman*. London: Hodder & Stoughton, 1910. 242.

Halliwell, James Orchard, ed. *The Thornton Romances. The Early English Metrical Romances of Perceval, Isumbras, Eglamour, and Degrevant*. London: John Bowyer Nichols & Son, 1844. 141.

The Holy Bible. King James Authorized Version. London: Barker, 1611.

Hume, Fergus. *Red Money*. New York: G. W. Dillingham, 1911. 6.

The Lay of Havelok the Dane. Ed. Walter W. Skeat. Early English Text Society. London: Kegan Paul, Trench, Trubner, 1868. 66–67.

Lewis, Sinclair. *Elmer Gantry*. New York: Harcourt, Brace, 1927. 366.

Macaulay, Rose. *Keeping up Appearances*. London: W. Collins, 1928. 57.

Macaulay, Thomas Babington. *The History of England from the Accession of James the Second*. Vol. 4. London: Longman, Brown, Green, and Longmans, 1855. 532.

More, Sir Thomas. *The Workes of Sir Thomas More*. London: Cawod, Waly, and Tottell, 1557. 339.

Scott, Sir Walter. *Ivanhoe: A Romance*. Boston: Houghton Mifflin, 1930. 172.

Shakespeare, William. *All's Well That Ends Well*. Ed. G. K. Hunter. Arden Edition. London: Methuen, 1959. V.iii.65–67.

————. *Henry IV, Part II*. Facsimile of the Andrew Wise 1600 edition. London: University Microfilms, 1964. II.ii.56–57.

————. *King Lear*. Facsimile of the Pied Bull Quarto, 1608. Shakespeare Quarto Facsimiles No. 1. London: Shakespeare Association & Sidgwick and Jackson, 1939. V.i.1–4.

————. *The Merchant of Venice*. Facsimile of the Thomas Heyes 1600 edition. London: Shakespeare Association & Sidgwick and Jackson, 1939. II.viii.31–32.

————. *Much Ado about Nothing*. Shakepeare Quarto Facsimiles No. 15. Oxford: Clarendon, 1971. III.ii.15–17.

————. *Othello*. Facsimile of the Thomas Walkley 1622 edition. London: University Microfilms, 1964. II.i.31–32.

————. *The Two Gentlemen of Verona*. Facsimile of the 1763 Edition. London: Cornmarket Press, 1969. III.i.44–45.

Shelley, Percy Bysshe. *The Cenci*. London: William Benbow, 1827. 10.

Sheridan, Richard Brinsley. "The Rivals." *Complete Works of Sheridan*. London: Chatto & Windus, 1897. 123.

Sir Orfeo. Ed. A. J. Bliss. 2nd ed. Oxford: Clarendon, 1966.

The Spectator. No. 133 (2 August 1711). Vol. 2. London: W. Gracie, 1807. 215.

Stevenson, Robert Louis. "An Apology for Idlers." *Virginibus Puerisque and Other Papers*. London: C. Kegan Paul, 1881. 123–24.

Tennyson, Alfred Lord. *The Poems of Tennyson*. Ed. Christopher Ricks. Longmans'Annotated English Poets. London: Longmans, Green, 1969. The May Queen, New Year's Eve, iv.

Thorpe, Benjamin, ed. *Ða Halgan Godspel On Englisc. The Anglo-Saxon Version of the Holy Gospels*. London: J. G. F. & J. Rivington, 1842.

Trollope, Anthony. *The Last Chronicle of Barset*. Vol. 2. London: Smith, Elder, 1867. 236.

Tuke, Sir Samuel. *The Adventures of Five Hours*. Ed. B. Van Thal. London: Robert Holden, 1927. I.i.

Vanbrugh, Sir John. ''The Relapse or Virtue in Danger.'' *The Complete Works of Sir John Vanbrugh*. Ed. Bonamy Dobree. Vol. 1. London: Nonesuch, 1927. II.1.

Westminster Gazette, no. 8080, 21. London: 1893 – 1927.

NOTES

1. The analysis is based on my University of California, Berkeley, dissertation, *Unified Theory of the English Subjunctive* (1980).
2. Two recent works on the English moods, Khlebnikova (1976) and Davies (1979), offer systemic analyses of the subjunctive which are quite different from the analysis proposed here.
3. See Delbrück (1897), Hirt (1934), Hahn (1953), Gonda (1956), and Lehmann (1974). These grammarians differ widely in their views on the original or basic meaning of the Indo-European optative. Delbrück argues that the optative means 'wish', and Hirt claims that it descends from a root meaning 'go'. Hahn believes that it is originally a future tense form, while Gonda feels that its basic meaning is 'contingency', and Lehmann thinks that its primary meaning is 'voluntative'.
4. For further discussion of formal criteria for determining subjunctive forms in present-day English, see Hirtle (1964) and Turner (1980). For discussion of formal criteria for determining subjunctive forms in Old English, see Behre (1934).
5. Harsh (1968) provides a statistical analysis documenting the decline of the subjunctive.
6. See, for instance, Sweet (1892: 105), Poutsma (1926: 9), Curme (1935: 389), and Jespersen (1954: 623).
7. I get this usage from Julian Boyd, who uses the terms to describe ambiguity in modal forms.
8. It is possible that each of these implications can be derived as a generalized conversational implicature in ways described by Grice (1975).
9. A questioned imperative may be given different interpretations. Two paraphrases of *Be early?* are "Do you want me to be early?" and "I want you to be early—is that all right with you?" In either case, the illocutionary force is different from the illocutionary force of commands, but the signification of the imperative mood remains constant.
10. Searle (1969: 68) makes the same point: "A man who says 'I (hereby) promise' not only promises, but *says* he does."

11. Page numbers here and throughout refer to Visser (1963–73). I supply glosses for sentences that may be difficult for modern speakers to interpret.
12. It is perhaps doubtful whether the stage direction is a clause, though if it is, the verb must be subjunctive. Jespersen (1954) says that the verb in such constructions is "originally subjunctive, hence without -s in the third person singular" (p. 63). He notes that the OED calls the verb a third person imperative (see OED under *enter*), but he comments, giving several examples, that in many cases the verb appears to function as an indicative (see pp. 625–26). For some further discussion of constructions like this, see Visser, pp. 807–8.
13. Searle (1983: 29–36), analyzing the nature of mental states such as hope and fear, comes to the same conclusion about manner of representation.
14. See Visser, p. 826. In citing examples, Visser points out that the object clauses in such sentences are much like clauses of result.
15. For a statistical study of the subjunctive in temporal clauses in Old English, see Callaway (1931).
16. For a statistical study of the subjunctive in clauses of purpose and result in Old English, see Callaway (1933).
17. Strawson (1952: 85 note) observes that one may use the past subjunctive when "simply working out the consequences of an hypothesis which one may be prepared eventually to accept". Karttunen and Peters (1977) argue that the 'counterfactual' sense, when it arises, is the result of a conversational implicature.
18. 'Imagined possibility' coincides with what Jespersen (1932: Chapters 9 and 10) calls the 'imaginative use of tenses'.
19. For an attested example, see Section 3.5.2: *I thought upon Antonio when he told me and wished in silence that it were not his.*
20. Although no examples with the word *wish* have come to hand, the assumption is quite safe, as it really involves no more than the assumption that the past subjunctive can signify past time. That it can is established by the following examples from *Ælfric's Grammar* (I supply the modern glosses):

> utinam legerem nunc
> ēalā gif ic rædde nū
> 'if only I were reading now'
> utinam legerem heri
> ēalā gif ic rædde gyrstan dæg
> 'if only I read (had read) yesterday'
> utinam legissem in iuuentute
> ēalā gif ic rædde on jugoðe
> 'if only I read (had read) in my youth'
>   Zupitza (1880: 125)

I assume that Latin *utinam legerem heri* and *utinam legissem heri* could also be translated into Old English as *ic wisce þæt ic rædde gyrstan dæg,* 'I wish that I had read yesterday', and there is certainly no reason to assume the contrary.

21. Visser does not provide an example in which the verb of the independent clause is present tense and the verb of the dependent clause is distinctively past subjunctive. Poutsma (1926: 179) cites the following example, how-ever: *It is time that a more reasonable distribution of the burdens of revenue were permanently established.*

22. Attested examples with a distinctively present subjunctive verb in the de-pendent clause are *Hit is tyme þat þou . . . be ioynede and felawechipede in þe noumbre of stronge menne* (Visser, p. 823) and *It's high time that the task be undertaken of promoting international good feeling* (Pout-sma 1926: 179).

23. Comparable sentences with a present indicative verb in the subordinate clause can be expanded in the same way: *He looks as if he is sick* be-comes "He looks as he looks if he is sick". The expanded version is grat-ingly repetitious, but it is readily interpretable. Roughly, it is equivalent to the sequence of sentences, "If he is sick, he looks a certain way. He looks just that way now."

24. For further discussion of the indeterminacy of *will,* see Boyd and Boyd (1980).

25. It is noteworthy, though, that a great many languages use a past tense form to express imagined possibility. Jespersen (1932: 114) points out that this use of the past tense is very common in the Indo-European family. For some discussion of this use of past tense forms as a crosslinguistic phenom-enon, see Steele (1975) and James (1982). It is conceivable that such usage in many if not all cases arises as I suggest it does in English by combination of the past tense form with a form signifying practical modality or with some other form or in some context which is forward-looking.

26. These examples and all others from French are taken from Daudon (1962).

27. These examples and all others from Greek are taken from Smyth (1956).

REFERENCES

Anscombe, G. E. M. (1957). *Intention*. Oxford: Clarendon Press.

Austin, J. L. (1962). *How To Do Things With Words*. Cambridge, MA: Harvard University Press.

Behre, Frank (1934). *The Subjunctive in Old English Poetry*. Göteborgs Högskolas Årsskrift 40. Göteborg: Wettergren & Kerbers Förlag.

Boyd, Julian, and J. P. Thorne (1969). "The Semantics of Modal Verbs". *Journal of Linguistics*, 5, 57–74.

Boyd, Julian, and Zelda Boyd (1980). "Shall and Will". In Leonard Michaels and Christopher Ricks, eds. *The State of the Language*. Berkeley: University of California Press.

Callaway, Morgan (1931). *The Temporal Subjunctive in Old English*. Austin: University of Texas Press.

————. (1933). *The Consecutive Subjunctive in Old English*. Boston: D. C. Heath.

Campbell, A. (1959). *Old English Grammar*. Oxford: Oxford University Press.

Chomsky, Noam (1957). *Syntactic Structures*. The Hague: Mouton.

————. (1965). *Aspects of the Theory of Syntax*. Cambridge, MA: M.I.T. Press.

Curme, G. O. (1935). *Syntax*. Boston: D. C. Heath.

Daudon, René (1962). *French in Review*. 2nd edition. New York: Harcourt, Brace and World.

Davies, Eirian C. (1979). *On the Semantics of Syntax*. London: Croom Helm.

Delbrück, Berthold (1897). *Vergleichende Syntax der Indogermanischen Sprachen*. Vol. 2. Strassburg: Karl J. Trübner.

Gonda, Jan (1956). *The Character of the Indo-European Moods*. Wiesbaden: Harrassowitz.

Grice, H. Paul (1975). "Logic and Conversation". In Peter Cole and Jerry L. Morgan, eds. *Syntax and Semantics 3: Speech Acts*. New York: Academic Press, pp. 41–58.

Hacking, Ian (1975). "All Kinds of Possibility". *Philosophical Review*, 84, 321–38.

Hahn, E. Adelaide (1953). *Subjunctive and Optative: Their Origin as Futures*. Lancaster, PA: American Philological Association.

Harris, James (1751). *Hermes*. London: J. Nourse and P. Vaillant.

Harsh, Wayne (1968). *The Subjunctive in English*. University, AL: University of Alabama Press.

Hirt, Hermann (1934). *Handbuch des Urgermanischen*. Vol. 3. Heidelberg: Carl Winter's Universitätsbuchhandlung.

Hirtle, W. H. (1964) "The English Present Subjunctive". *Canadian Journal of Linguistics*, 9, 75 – 82.

James, Deborah (1982). "Past Tense and the Hypothetical: A Crosslinguistic Study". *Studies in Language*, 6, 375 – 403.

James, Francis (1980). *Unified Theory of the English Subjunctive*. University of California, Berkeley, dissertation.

Jespersen, Otto (1932). *A Modern English Grammar*. Vol. 4. London: G. Allen and Unwin.

— — — —. (1954). *A Modern English Grammar*. Vol. 7. London: G. Allen and Unwin.

Karttunen, Lauri, and Stanley Peters (1977). "Requiem for Presupposition". In Kenneth Whistler et al., eds. *Proceedings of the Third Annual Meeting of the Berkeley Linguistics Society*. Berkeley: Berkeley Linguistics Society.

Khlebnikova, Irina B. (1976). *The Conjunctive Mood in English*. The Hague: Mouton.

Lehmann, Winfred P. (1974). *Proto-Indo-European Syntax*. Austin: University of Texas Press.

Oxford English Dictionary (OED). Compact Edition (1971). Oxford: Oxford University Press.

Poutsma, Hendrik (1926). *A Grammar of Late Modern English*. Vol. 2:2. Groningen: P. Noordhof.

Searle, John R. (1969). *Speech Acts*. Cambridge: Cambridge University Press.

— — — —. (1972). "A Taxonomy of Illocutionary Acts". In Keith Gunderson, ed. *Minnesota Studies in the Philosophy of Science*. Vol. 7. Minneapolis: University of Minnesota Press, pp. 344 – 69.

— — — —. (1983). *Intentionality*. Cambridge: Cambridge University Press.

Smyth, H. W. (1956). *Greek Grammar*. Cambridge, MA: Harvard University Press.

Steele, Susan (1975). "Past and Irrealis: Just What Does It all Mean". *International Journal of American Linguistics*, 41, 200 – 217.

Strawson, P. F. (1952). *Introduction to Logical Theory*. London: Methuen.

Sweet, Henry (1892). *New English Grammar*. Vol. 1. Oxford: Clarendon Press.

Turner (1980). "The Marked Subjunctive in Contemporary English". *Studia Neophilologica*, 52, 271 – 277.

Visser, F. Th. (1963–73). *An Historical Syntax of the English Language*. 4 vol. Leiden: E. J. Brill.

Zupitza, Julius (1880). *Ælfrics Grammatik und Glossar*. Reprint. Berlin: Max Niehans Verlag, 1966.

INDEX